Love Without Measure

Love Without Measure

Extracts from the Writings of
St Bernard of Clairvaux

Introduced and arranged by

PAUL DIEMER

Cistercian Publications
Kalamazoo, Michigan

First published in 1990 by
Darton, Longman and Todd Ltd
89 Lillie Road, London SW6 1UD

Introduction and arrangement
© 1990 Paul Diemer

ISBN 0 87907 727 1

Love Without Measure is No. 127 in the
Cistercian Studies Series.

Phototypeset by Input Typesetting Ltd, London SW19 8DR
Printed and bound in Great Britain by
Courier International Ltd, Tiptree, Essex

For P.M.D.

Contents

Acknowledgements

Extracts are used by permission of the following publishers: *The Works of Bernard of Clairvaux* and *Thomas Merton on St Bernard*: Cistercian Publications, Michigan; *The Letters of St Bernard of Clairvaux*, translated by Bruno Scott James: Burns and Oates Ltd; *On Loving God* by Bernard of Clairvaux, edited by Hugh Martin: SCM Press.

Chronology

1090   Born at the castle of Fontaines-les-Dijon in Burgundy.

1112   Entered the monastery of Citeaux with a group of friends and relatives.

1115   Sent as Abbot to found the monastery of Clairvaux.

1118   Suffered a severe illness, the effects of which were always with him.

1118–   During Bernard's abbacy 68 daughter houses founded
1153   by Clairvaux.

1124   Severe famine in the district. Bernard writes his first treatise: *The Steps of Humility and Pride*.

1126   Wrote his treatises *On Loving God* and *Grace and Free-choice*.

1130   Schism in the papacy. For eight years Bernard worked and journeyed to heal the schism. The result was a masterpiece of statecraft.

1132   Sent a group of monks to England to found the Abbey of Rievaulx.

1135   Bernard present at Council of Pisa. From this date until his death he worked on the *Sermons on the Song of Songs*.

1139   Friendship with Malachy, Archbishop of Armagh.

1146   Bernard preached the second Crusade at Vezelay, and defended the Jews. Present at the Diet of Spires.

1147   Home at Clairvaux.

1148   Failure of the Crusade.

1149–   Wrote his treatise *De Consideratione* for the Cistercian
1153   Pope Eugene III.

1153   Died at Clairvaux.

1174   Canonised by Pope Alexander III.

Introduction: The Man and his Message

'Bernard, Bernard, why have you come here?' This was a question St Bernard used to ask himself every day when he was a novice at Citeaux.

One answer to the question seems to be expressed in Ribalta's painting of Christ embracing St Bernard from the cross. Bernard is completely absorbed, out of this world, a weary traveller come home after a long journey. Christ is leaning from his cross, the marks of his agony all about him. Here is both the agony and the ecstasy; a being with Christ, or rather a union with the Word enfleshed in Christ.

The painting expresses the culmination of a relationship which according to Bernard's teaching was at the heart of the Cistercian/monastic life. He saw the focal point of this relationship as love. It is love that gives meaning to the monastic life. A love that is like the sunlight, not only giving light but warmth, not only enabling a person to endure and to bear, but also to rejoice. Love unites, and union through love means a union of wills, for the will is the means by which we become loving persons. So Bernard set himself to sort out the tangle of different kinds of loves and desires that drew his will this way and that. This is what the monastic life is for, and it is a lifetime's work.

The Bernard who entered Citeaux was an exceptionally gifted and talented young man, and he realised that developing his relationship with Christ was not quite the same thing as developing his gifts and potentialities, and that his choice to become a monk would impose limitations: his vocation would have to be ratified again and again, day after day. Considering his gifts, it must have been a struggle at times – but in spite of his absences from his monastery on behalf of the Church he always remained at heart a monk and a Cistercian.

Bernard was, above all, profoundly Christian, soaked in the mysteries of Christ and in the doctrine of St Paul. Inviting Thomas of Beverley to enter Clairvaux, he writes: 'Perhaps you will say that it is too late, and that you are a sinner. All right, so am I; and I am not put off by another sinner. I do not turn away from someone who is ill; for I know that I am ill too. Nor do I worry about the gravity of the sickness, when I think of the skill of the Doctor and of his pity and compassion which is so well known to me.' He repeats what he never tires of saying, 'Remember, no matter how great your sins, how bad your conscience, how dissolute your youth or mis-spent your life, yet you shall be cleansed, restored, renewed. Come and see, come and choose the best part that eye has not seen nor ear heard.' He explains that Jesus brings a message from his Father which he whispers to his friends – the message that we are each called from all eternity – and linked with this call, is the mercy of God which has no beginning, no end. It is a call to become a child of God, to be one's true self, a call to love.

Bernard has a very rich doctrine on the Spirit of love, the Holy Spirit, and says that it is the Holy Spirit who gives us both the courage to believe that God loves us, and the power to love in return – the Spirit, as it were, provides the love. This, he says is the secret that Jesus passes on to his own, and the voice that tells us this is heard only with the ears of the heart; not in public, in the market place but in private – apart. 'So, come to Clairvaux and accept me as your fellow-disciple and we will both have one master, Christ, who is the end and meaning of the Law.' To another he writes, 'Come, if you want to grasp Christ, do not simply read about him but follow him. He stands before your eyes crying, "Whoever thirsts let him come to me and drink and I will refresh you." Are you afraid you will break down when Truth himself promises to refresh you?'

His letters show many facets of his personality; we see him very busy with those who have consulted him, preoccupied and tired out when dealing with matters of the Church and the monasteries under his care, and apt to get worked up if he feels the good of the Church is at stake. On the occasion of a controversial election of a new Archbishop at York, he writes to the Curia at Rome: 'I am on fire! I tell you I am so consumed that I am weary of life. What incredible rashness! A man publicly infamous has become a Bishop – not consecrated I say but execrated.' Yet he writes on the very same matter to Abbot William of Rievaulx, his former secretary, 'I am writing to console you, for your zeal is well known to me and it would ill become our Order and not help your House if this zeal were to flare up beyond the bounds of prudence and discretion – so bear it calmly'!

He could be infinitely kind and human, as when he wrote to the parents of one young monk: 'Do not worry about him, I will be a mother and father, both a brother and sister to him.' He could be sensitive and understanding and knew how to wait, as when he persuaded the contemplative and spiritually perceptive Richard of Fountains to continue in office although from the very beginning he had had another Yorkshireman in mind to be Abbot of this new monastery.

Bernard especially gave support and encouragement. He encouraged Abbot Roger of Byland not to resign, even though he felt like an old man while he was still in his forties. Then, tongue in cheek, he suggested that Roger's successors might have smaller estates. (It was in fact another 40 years before Roger finally resigned, by then aged over 90!)

He also encouraged, and even ordered, the young Aelred of Rievaulx to write his masterpiece *The Mirror of Charity*, and gave his friendship and support to Abbot Robert of Newminster who had been misrepresented and libelled by some of his community.

Though not strong physically, he persevered as a young monk with manual work, but ruined his health by fasting and penance, and we get a hint of his ill-health when he writes about visiting England: 'I wait and wait but up till now I have been prevented. The way is hard and difficult and my body is weak.' He went on to add that the journeys he had to make for the business of the brethren and the cause of the Church were like a heavy burden – but these journeys always led him back to his beloved Clairvaux.

There seems to have been something quite unique about the Clairvaux of Bernard's day. Many of the brethren sent to distant foundations wanted to return there to die. At first the buildings were poor and cramped, and when after some years the prior presented Bernard with some plans for a new monastery, his first reaction was the human, 'What will people say?' The life there was austere. The sight of the brethren working together in silence made William of St Thierry think of solitaries in community. But it was a real community, for Bernard had a genius for inspiring affection among the brothers, and said that one of the worst evils to which man can succumb is to be without affection. The brothers were concerned about one another, and ready to complain to Bernard if they thought he had treated one of them unjustly. He, on his part, insisted that they must be bound together not only by a life-stream of a shared love, but also by a shared will, a common ideal and purpose – a basic 'common will' as he called it, from which no one should opt out.

It was from his study of the Bible and of the Fathers of the Church, as well as from his knowledge of men and his own experience, that he learnt of God's unconditional love and goodness, and of his care for us sinners. He wrote of this in his treatises and sermons, and especially in his master-piece – *Sermons on the Song of Songs* – where we can find a summary of his entire spiritual teaching.

He explains that we were made in the image and likeness of God, but through sin the likeness has been lost and the image defaced. Our life's work is to renew and restore this image. We still retain our free will, but natural effort on our part is not enough by itself and we cannot save ourselves. First we need humility. This is the foundation, the ability, which is itself a grace, to recognise both our spiritual weakness and the love and power that God is offering to us. Then we must go further, accept our dependence and place our lives in his love and care. This is humility in action; it demands a reorientation of our self-love, a return of love to its source. It is love that is at the heart of our return to God.

Bernard also points out the need for faith – to bring us through those dry and monotonous periods of life when we are tempted to grow weary of well-doing. At such times, he says, we need the help of the Holy Spirit, who comes to dwell with us and gives a zest, a savour, a taste to our good works.

Bernard belongs to a different age and culture to ours, and we may not always find him easy to read. His approach to Scripture, his use of symbolism, and his play on words are sometimes not to our taste; but if we look only for ways of thought that are familiar to us, we may miss much of value that he offers when he speaks of the basic human and spiritual experiences that he and his contemporaries share with us today.

His whole approach is eminently biblical – showing us God's healing power bending down to raise us from the gutter to the closest union with the Word, and calling from us a deep radical trust that goes out to meet the incomprehensible goodness of Jesus who has made us his own.

1

The Mystery of Christ

The spiritual teaching of St Bernard is really the spiritual theology of the Mystery of Christ. It has its roots in his teaching on the Blessed Trinity. God, he says, lives by a law – the law of love; the law of love which holds together the Three Persons binding them in the bond of peace. This love, which is God himself, reaches down to draw all mankind to union with himself. It is God's gift to us making us like him, and it stamps our souls not only with a desire for him but with his desire for us.

> *This is the love I mean*
> *Not our love for God*
> *But God's love for us. (1 Jn)*

With the Fall, the original bonds between God and his creation began to disintegrate. There now existed in the human personality a conflict between good and evil, as we ourselves know when we look into our own hearts. Above all, our relationship with God, our Creator and Father, had been broken and neither we ourselves nor our first parents could restore it.

We are sinners unable to reach God by our own efforts, so the Blessed Trinity, overflowing with goodness, was ready to send the Word as our Saviour when the time had come. With the Incarnation of the Word, God was in his world making ordinary human living the vehicle of salvation and leaving a pattern for us all to follow; and then through his cross and passion, resurrection and ascension, leading the human race back to the side of his Father. Above all, God is still with his world, loving us, seeking us and waiting to be found.

This is the heart of Bernard's message. It may be truly said that the following quotations from his works do not do him justice

1

removed as they are from their setting of biblical and liturgical allusions, and often his sense of style, play on words, and sometimes his sheer poetry have been lost. In spite of this, something of his genius does shine through; something of his sensitivity; something of his utter self-gift as a lover of Christ and a man of God.

What the Blessed Trinity has Done for Us

In the beginning he created all things with power, and he governed all things with wisdom, and men had clear evidence of the divine power and wisdom in the creation and conservation of the universe. There was goodness in God – goodness exceeding great. As yet it lay hidden in the heart of the Father, ready to be poured out at the proper time on the children of Adam.

Even then the Lord was thinking thoughts of peace, of sending to us him who is our peace, so that he might give us peace upon peace. So, his own loving-kindness induced the Word of God, enthroned on high to come down to us. His mercy drew him down, his fidelity to his promise to visit us kept him here, and the spotless womb of the Virgin received him.

O Mother of God, O Sovereign Lady of the world all generations shall call you blessed, because to all generations you have given life and glory. For in you the angels shall for ever find gladness, the just grace, and sinners pardon. Rightly are the eyes of all the world directed towards you, since it is in you and through you and from you that the kindly hand of the Almighty has renewed what he originally created.

Charity is the Law of God

When a person keeps nothing of their own for themselves, everything they have is God's, and what is God's cannot be unclean. Therefore the unspotted law of God is charity, which seeks not what may benefit itself, but what may benefit many. Charity is called the law of the Lord either because the Lord himself lives by it or else because none other may have it except by his gift.

What else but charity preserves that supreme and unspeakable unity in the Blessed Trinity? Charity is therefore a law, and it is a law of the Lord, holding together, as it were, the Trinity and binding it in the bond of peace. Charity is the divine substance itself.

God is charity. It follows that charity can be correctly said to be both God and the gift of God. That charity gives charity, the substance of charity, the quality of charity. When we speak of the giver we mean the substance; when we speak of the gift we mean the quality.

Nothing is left without law, since even the Law of all things is not without a law, yet a law not other than itself for, although it did not create itself, it nevertheless rules itself.

The Law of the Slave

The slave and the hireling also have a law, a law not from God, but which they make for themselves; the one by not loving God, and the other by loving something more than God. They have a law, but a law of their own, not of God, yet a law which is subject to the law of God. Anyone can make law for himself, but he cannot withdraw it from the order of the eternal law.

But anyone who thus makes a law for himself is trying to imitate his Creator by ruling himself, and making his own self-will a law for himself, just as God is his own law and subject only to himself.

What a heavy and insupportable burden this is. He is bowed down and bent under it. When he says: 'I am become burdensome to myself,' he shows that he has been a law unto himself, and that no other than he himself has done this. It is the property of the eternal law of God that anyone who will not be ruled sweetly by God, shall be ruled as a punishment by himself. He, who of his own will throws off the sweet and light yoke of charity shall unwillingly suffer the insupportable burden of his own self-will.

Christ our Saviour

It was our need of him that induced him to visit us, and the greatness of that need is clearly indicated by the greatness of his condescension. Just as the gravity of the disease may be inferred from the costliness of the medicines used for its cure, so too may we know the number of our ailments from the many remedies provided for us.

For our Saviour is a faithful Counsellor, who can never deceive us or be deceived; he is a strong helper whom labour never wearies, he is a mighty protector who will quickly enable us to trample underfoot the power of Satan. For he is the wisdom of God, who is ever ready to instruct the ignorant; he is the power of God, to whom it is so easy to strengthen the weak and rescue those in danger. Therefore my brethren, in all our doubts and perplexities let us have recourse to so wise a Master. In all our undertakings let us invoke the assistance of so powerful a helper. In our every combat let us commit our souls to the keeping of so faithful a protector. He has come into the world for this purpose, that living here in us with us and for us, he might illumine our darkness, lighten our labours, and guard us from all dangers.

Our Need of Christ

Without doubt the whole human race labours under a three-fold misery, which painfully oppresses everyone who lives in this region of the shadow of death, subject to the infirmities of the flesh and the assaults of temptation. For we are easily led astray; we soon weary of labour; we quickly yield to violence. We are deceived when we try to discern between good and evil; we faint and give up as often as we undertake a good work; if we try to resist evil, we are promptly cast down and overcome.

Very necessary therefore is the coming of the Saviour. Very necessary is the presence of Christ for us so surrounded by dangers. God grant that he may not only come to us, but that he may also dwell in us by faith to enlighten our blindness. That he may remain with us by grace to assist our utter impotence, and stand by us with his power to protect and defend our fragility. If he remains with us surely we can do all things in him who strengthens us. If he is for us who can be against us?

The Time of our Saviour's Coming

We must now think for a moment about the time at which our Saviour comes, for as you know it was not at the beginning, nor in the middle, but at the end of the ages that he came to us.

Truly the day was already far spent and the evening drawing near; the sun of justice was already beginning to set, and its rays now gave diminished light and warmth to the earth. The light of the knowledge of God had grown feeble, and as sin increased, charity grew cold. Angels no longer appeared to men, no prophet raised his voice; it seemed as though, overcome by the great hardness and obstinacy of men, they had ceased to intervene in human affairs. Then it was that the Son of God said: 'Here am I.'

Eternity broke in upon the world at the moment when temporal prosperity was at its height. For to give only one example, peace among nations was at that time so universal that at a single man's bidding it was possible to carry out a census of the whole world.

The Road by which the Saviour Comes

Now we must earnestly search out the road by which he comes, so that we may be able to go out to meet him as is fitting. However, as he came once on earth in visible flesh to work out our redemption, so he comes daily in a hidden spiritual way to save each individual soul. This spiritual coming of his is shown to be hidden in the text: 'Under his shadow we shall live among the nations.' So, then, surely even if the sick man is unable to go very far to meet such a great Physician, he should at least make an effort to lift his head and raise himself up a little to greet him as he approaches.

It is not necessary for you to cross the seas, nor to pierce the clouds, nor to climb mountains to meet your God. It is not a lengthy road that is set before you; you have only to enter into yourself to find him. 'For his word is very near you; it is on your lips and in your heart.'

Encounter him in compunction of heart and in confession of your sins, so that you may at least leave behind you the dunghill of a defiled conscience, for the Author of purity could not be asked to enter such a place.

But I should like to know the reason why he has come to us, and why we did not rather go to him. For it is we who have need of him not he of us. Thus, among men, it is not the custom of the rich to visit the poor, even when they wish to give them help. My Brothers, it were more fitting that we should go to him than that he should come to us.

But there were two obstacles: in the first place our eyes were weak and dim, whereas he dwells in light inaccessible. Secondly we were as the paralytic lying helpless in his bed, and could not by any means attain to the loftiness of the divine majesty. Therefore, our most kind Saviour, the tender physician of our souls, came down from his throne on high and tempered his glory's splendour to the weakness of our vision. For he, the brightness of eternal light, enclosed himself in the lantern, so to speak, of that glorious flesh which he took from a virgin mother, and which is clearly signified by that light and luminous cloud upon which, Isaiah says, the Lord was to ascend, so that he might come down into Egypt.

Why the Son of God came to Us

The purpose must surely be something great, since the mercy is so great, and the kindness so great, and so great too the love. The Lord came down in haste from the heavenly hills to seek the one sheep of his hundred which had strayed from the fold . . . that hundredth sheep which as the Gospel tells us wandered from the fold. That sheep my Brothers, represents the human race which the loving-kind Shepherd comes in quest of, leaving his other ninety-nine sheep on the mountains.

Oh, how marvellous a condescension in God to come down from heaven in quest of the children of men! And how great an honour for us to be sought by God! Not that we seem to be anything of ourselves, but because he who made us has made so much of us.

For all the riches of the world, and whatever else it possesses which the human heart can desire, all this is little, indeed it is nothing at all in comparison with the honour of being sought after by God. O Lord, what is man that you should exalt him? Or why do you set your heart upon him?

2

Love

Love is the golden thread running through all Bernard's teaching, and, as Thomas Merton pointed out, it is not something that can somehow be profitably fitted into man's life. It is man's whole reason for existing and until he begins to love God he does not really begin to live. So Bernard discusses our obligation to love God and Christ, and what should be the measure of our love; to love without measure with a self-giving love that never withdraws itself.

Love, he says, is a great reality returning to its source, seeking the fountainhead so as to draw afresh and flow ever more freely. Here is insight indeed! Cistercian monasteries were consequently called 'schools of charity' (gymnasia where it could be exercised and developed) for it has to be lived out in faith in the rough and tumble of daily life. We know from experience that our wants, our desires, our loves become tangled and get out of hand. Our love needs to be 'set in order'. So the great work of our lives is to set the compass of our love towards God and he himself will help us to purify it.

In his treatise 'On the Love of God', and in his letter to Guy the Carthusian Prior, Bernard speaks of the four degrees of love, showing that it belongs to man's very nature to love – he was born to love – but because of the Fall his love has become selfish, and to some extent will always remain so in this life.

Love unites the lover with what he loves, and ultimately it has to do with an act of the will going out to enjoy and to rest in something or someone as its last end. The 'last end' for a human person is God, and if we enjoy creatures, rest in them in this way, then we are untrue to our deepest selves. We are made for God, and the soul that loves creatures in this way becomes like the things that it loves, and thus unlike its true self – and unlike God.

It is in Christ that we see love at its strongest and most beautiful. He loved his Father utterly and ourselves to the utmost.

Love

Love is sufficient for itself; it gives pleasure to itself and for its own sake. It is its own merit and its own reward. Love needs no cause beyond itself, nor does it demand fruits; it is its own purpose. I love because I love; I love that I may love. Love is a great reality; and if it returns to its beginning and goes back to its origin, seeking its source again, it will always draw afresh from it and thereby flow freely.

Love is the only one of the motions of the soul, of its senses and affections, in which the creature can respond to its Creator (even if not as an equal) and repay his favour in some similar way.

When God loves, he desires nothing but to be loved, since he loves us for no other reason than to be loved, for he knows that those who love are blessed in their very love.

How God Should be Loved

Consider first how God merits to be loved, that there is to be no limit to that love, for he loved us first. Such a one loved us so much and so freely, insignificant as we are and such as we are, that as I said at the beginning, we must love God without any limit.

Finally as love offered to God has for object the one who is immeasurable and infinite – what I ask, should be the aim or degree of our love? What about the fact that our love is not given gratuitously but in payment of a debt? God whose greatness knows no end, to whose wisdom there is no limit, whose peace exceeds all understanding, loves – and we think we can requite him with some measure of love?

My God, my help, I shall love you as much as I am able for your gift. My love is less than is your due, yet not less than I am able, for if I cannot love you as much as I should, still I cannot love you more than I can. I shall only be able to love you more when you give me more, although you can never find my love worthy of you.

Why We Should Love God

You want me to tell you why God is to be loved and how much. The reason for loving God is God himself: and the measure of love due to him is immeasurable love. He gave himself for us unworthy wretches. Hence, if one seeks for God's claim upon our love here is the chiefest: because he first loved us.

Ought he not to be loved in return, when we think who loved, whom he loved, and how much he loved? For whom was such unutterable love made manifest? The Apostle tells us: 'When we were his enemies, we were reconciled to God by the death of his Son'. So it was God who loved us, loved us freely, and loved us while we were yet enemies.

And how great was this love of his? St John answers: 'God so loved the world that he gave his only begotten Son, that whosoever believes in him should not perish, but have everlasting life'. St Paul adds: 'He did not spare his own Son but delivered him up for us all'. And the Son says of himself: 'Greater love no man has than this, that a man lay down his life for his friends'. This is the claim that God the holy, the supreme, the omnipotent, has upon men, defiled and base and weak.

Christ First Loved Us

Good Jesus, the chalice you drank, the price of our redemption, makes me love you more than all the rest. This alone would be enough to claim our love. This I say is what wins our love so sweetly, justly demands it, firmly binds it, deeply affects it. Our Saviour had to toil so hard in this, in fact in making the whole world the Creator did not labour so much.

In the beginning he spoke and they were made; he commanded and they were created. But in saving us he had to endure men who contradicted his words, criticised his actions, ridiculed his sufferings, and mocked his death. See how much he loved us. Add to this fact that he was not returning love but freely offering it. For who had given him anything first, that it should be returned to him? As St John said: 'Not that we had loved him, but that he had first loved us.'

He loved us even before we existed, and in addition he loved us when we resisted him. According to St Paul: 'Even when we were still his enemies we were reconciled to God through the blood of his Son.' If he had not loved his enemies, he could not have had any friends, just as he would have had no one to love if he had not loved those who were not.

How We Ought to Love Christ

Christian, learn from Christ how you ought to love Christ. Learn a love that is tender, wise, and strong; love with tenderness not passion, with wisdom not foolishness, and with strength, lest you become weary and turn away from the love of the Lord. Do not let the glory of the world or the pleasures of the flesh lead you astray; the wisdom of Christ should become sweeter to you than these. The light of Christ should shine so much for you that the spirit of lies and deceit will not seduce you.

Finally, Christ as the strength of God should support you so that you may not be worn down by difficulties. Let love enkindle your zeal, let knowledge inform it, let constancy strengthen it. Keep it fervent, discreet, courageous. See it is not tepid, or fearful, or timid.

So love the Lord your God with the full and deep affection of your heart, love him with your mind wholly awake and discreet, love him with all your strength, so much so that you would not even fear to die for love of him. Your affection for your Lord Jesus should be both tender and intimate, to oppose the sweet enticements of sensual life. Sweetness conquers sweetness as one nail drives out another.

Degrees of Love

Love is a great reality; but there are degrees to it. I suspect the love which seems to be founded on some hope of gain. It is weak, for if the hope of gain is removed it may be extinguished, or at least diminished. It is not pure, as it desires some return. Pure love has no self interest. Pure love does not gain strength through expectation, nor is it weakened through distrust.

This is the love of the Bride . . . Love is the being and hope of a bride. She is full of it, and the bridegroom is content with it. He asks nothing else, and she has nothing else to give. That is why he is the bridegroom and she is the bride; this love is the property only of the couple. No-one else can share it, not even a son.

True Love

God is not loved without a reward, although he should be loved without regard for one. True charity cannot be worthless, but as it does not seek its own advantage, it cannot be termed mercenary. Love pertains to the will, it is not a transaction; it cannot acquire or be acquired by a pact. It moves us freely, and it makes us spontaneous. True love is content with itself; it has its reward, the object of its love. Whatever you seem to love because of something else, you do not really love. You really love the end pursued and not that by which it is pursued . . .

True love merits its own reward, it does not seek it. A reward is offered him who does not yet love; but it is due to him who loves, and it is given to him who perseveres . . .

The soul that loves God seeks no other reward than the God whom it loves. Were the soul to demand anything else, then it would certainly love that other thing and not God.

Steps in our Love for God

Because we are flesh and blood born of the desire of the flesh, our desire or love must start in the flesh, and it will then if properly directed, progress under grace until it is fulfilled in the spirit.

At first a person loves himself for his own sake. He is flesh and is able only to know himself. But when he sees that he cannot subsist of himself, then he begins by faith to seek and love God as necessary for himself. And so in the second stage he loves God, not yet for God's sake, but for his own sake. However when on account of his own necessity, he begins to meditate, read, pray and obey, he becomes accustomed little by little to know God and consequently to delight in him.

When he has tasted and seen how sweet is the Lord he passes to the third stage wherein he loves God for God's sake and not for his own. And here he remains, for I doubt whether the fourth stage has ever been fully reached in this life by any man. The stage that is, wherein a man loves himself only for God's sake.

3

Our Lady

*St Bernard was among the first to call Mary 'Domina Nostra' –
Our Lady. She is also the Star of the Sea whose light and protection
can save us from shipwreck. She is the Star of Jacob, the Royal
Road by which our Saviour came to us. Let us go to him through
her.*

*But we see her true position in the plan of Salvation, in the
mystery of Christ, in a dramatic passage on the Annunciation when
Bernard describes how not only the Angel waits for her reply, but
the whole of creation – right back to Adam. The whole world
awaits her answer; on it depends the coming of the Saviour for the
entire human race.*

*She is our Mother for she gives us Jesus our Brother. She is the
aqueduct who gives us water from the fountain of life springing up
in the very heart of the Father. She is the model for monks for she
reaches to the Godhead by her burning desire, her pure prayer, her
humility and her seeking – the very things they are striving for.
May her fragrance cling to our gifts as they are offered through her
hands. In a number of sermons not specifically on Our Lady, he
mentions her to illustrate the particular point he is making.*

*Not for nothing did Dante call him 'Mary's Bernard', and in his
great vision of Paradise it is Bernard the contemplative who leads
the poet to the side of Mary. She smiles on him, and kneeling there
he follows her eyes as she gazes on the glory of the Godhead and
sees within it the outline of a Man. She has shown him the blessed
fruit of her womb.*

Mary our Advocate

You have already realised, I suppose, that the Virgin herself is the royal road by which the Saviour came to us. Therefore, dear Brothers, let us endeavour to ascend by it to Jesus, who by the same way has come down to us. Let us strive, I say, to go by Mary to share his grace who by Mary came to share our misery. Through you O most blessed One, Finder of grace, Mother of life, Mother of salvation, through you let us have access to your Son, so that through you he may receive us, He who was given us through you.

Let your purity excuse before him the foulness of our corruption. Let your humility, so pleasing to God, make amends and obtain pardon for our pride. Let your abounding love cover the multitude of our sins. Let your glorious fecundity supply on our behalf for a fecundity of merit. O you who are Our Lady, our Mediatrix, and our Advocate, reconcile us to your Son. Grant, O most blessed One, that he who by your consent and co-operation, made himself a sharer of our poverty and weakness may by your intercession make us sharers of his own glory and happiness.

The Annunciation

Behold, Mary, the Angel now awaits your answer. We also, await from your lips the sentence of mercy and compassion. For, the price of our salvation is now offered to you: if you will only consent, we shall at once be set at liberty. Adam, now exiled from paradise with all his miserable offspring, implores this favour of you. For this Abraham entreats you, for this David, for this all the other holy fathers, your own ancestors, who are now dwelling in the shadow of death. See the whole world prostrate at your feet, awaits your answer.

For on your word depends the consolation of the desolate, the redemption of the captives, the pardon of the condemned, the salvation of all the children of Adam, of the entire human race.

O Virgin do not delay to answer. Speak the word which all on earth, all in limbo, and even all in paradise are waiting to hear. Christ himself, the King and Lord of all, longs for your answer.

Make haste, to answer the Angel, or rather to answer the Lord through the Angel. Say the word and receive the Word.

Mary's Consent

O, Blessed Virgin speak your human word and conceive the Divine Word. Pronounce the transitory word and embrace the everlasting Word.

Why do you hesitate? What do you fear? Believe, consent, and receive into your womb the Word of the Father. Let your humility take courage, let your modesty be confident. O, happy Virgin, open your heart to faith, open your lips to consent, open your bosom to your Creator.

Behold the Desired of all nations is standing outside and knocking at your door. Oh, if he should pass by while you delay to open. Arise therefore, and make haste to open to him. Arise by faith, make haste by devotion, open by consent.

'And Mary said: Behold the handmaid of the Lord, be it done to me according to your word.'

Star of the Sea

Mary means star of the sea, and the name suits the Virgin Mother. Rightly she is likened to a star, for as a star sends forth its ray without loss to itself, so does the Virgin bear her Son without hurt to herself; and as the ray detracts not from the brightness of the star, so likewise Mary's Son takes nothing from his Mother's innocence. She is that noble Star of Jacob, whose Ray gives light to all the world, the Ray whose splendour shines in heaven and penetrates to hell.

She is that star I say, uplifted over the ocean of this world, shining by her merit and shedding light on us by her example. O you who struggle in this stormy sea, do not turn your eyes from this star, if you would escape shipwreck! When the winds of temptation arise and you run on the rocks of tribulation, look at that star, think of Mary, call on her by name. If you follow her, you will not go off course; if you cry to her, you will not give up hope; if you think of her, you will not go astray. So will your own experience teach you how rightly it is said that 'the Virgin's name was Mary'.

The Second Eve

See the counsel of God; acknowledge the counsel of his wisdom, the counsel of his love. Planning to irrigate the whole ground with heavenly dew, the Lord first poured down upon the fleece this precious dew. Planning to redeem the human race he placed the whole ransom in the hands of Mary. Why was this? Possibly that Mother Eve might be exonerated by her daughter, and that the complaint of the man against the woman might be silenced for ever. Never again, Adam, will you be able to point your finger, and say to God, 'The woman whom you gave me to be my companion gave me of the forbidden fruit.' But rather, in future, say: 'The woman whom you gave me fed me with the fruit of heavenly blessings.'

Here indeed we have a counsel full of love. What I have told you is undoubtedly true, yet, unless I am mistaken it is not enough to satisfy you. You have enjoyed the sweetness of the milk, perhaps if we work a little longer we shall succeed in making butter. Let us therefore look more deeply and see with what tender devotion the Lord would have us honour Mary.

For Our Lady's Birthday

Life everlasting! A never failing fountain which irrigates the whole extent of the paradise of God. Now what is this fountain of life if it be not Christ the Lord? This stream from the heavenly source descends to us through an Aqueduct. It does not show all the fulness of the fountain, but it moistens our dry and withered hearts with some few drops of grace, giving more to one, less to another. The Aqueduct is always full, so that all may receive of its fulness.

You must have already guessed, dear brethren, to whom I allude under the image of an Aqueduct, which receiving the fulness of the Fountain from the Father's heart has passed it on to us, at least in so far as we could contain it. You know it was she to whom it was said, 'Hail full of grace'.

But how did this Conduit of ours, attain to the loftiness of the Fountain? How indeed, except by the ardour of her desires, by the fervour of her devotion, by the purity of her prayer? How did she reach up even to the inaccessible majesty but by knocking, by asking, by seeking? And she found what she was seeking since it was said to her, 'You have found grace with God.'

Mary gives us Jesus our Brother

Exercising a motherly care for us her poor children, in all things and through all things, the Virgin Mother calms our trembling fear, enlivens our faith, supports our hope, drives away our distrust, strengthens our timidity.

You were afraid, Adam, to approach the Father; you were terrified at the mere sound of his voice, and tried to hide among the trees. Therefore he gave you Jesus as your Mediator. What shall such a Son not be able to obtain for you from such a fatherly Father? Without doubt he will be heard for his reverence for the Father loves the Son.

Surely you are not afraid to approach Jesus also? He is your Brother and your flesh, tempted in all things as you are, yet without sin, so that he might have compassion. And this Brother has been given to us by Mary.

And so, whatsoever you have a mind to offer to the Lord, be sure to entrust it to Mary, so that your gift shall return to the Giver of all grace through the same channel by which you obtained it.

Mary, the Garden

The Lord has placed in Mary the fulness of all good. So that if there is anything of hope in us, if anything of grace, if anything of salvation, we may feel assured it has overflowed into us from her. Truly may we call her a garden of delights, which the divine 'South Wind' not merely comes and blows upon, but comes down into and blows through, causing the fragrance of its spices, that is, the precious gifts of heavenly grace to flow out and be spread around on every side.

Take away from the sky the sun which enlightens the world and what becomes of the day? Take away Mary, this Star of life's vast and spacious sea, and what is left to us but a cloud of swirling gloom and a thick and dense darkness? Therefore, my Brothers, with every fibre of our being, every feeling of our hearts, with all the affections of our minds, and with all the ardour of our souls, let us honour Mary, because such is the will of God, who would have us obtain everything through her hands. Such I say is the will of God who intends it for our benefit.

4

Made in God's Image and Likeness

The human soul was created in God's image and likeness. At the Fall it lost its likeness to its Creator; but the image remains, deformed but inseparable from the very essence of the soul.

This image consists in three things: man's natural simplicity, his natural immortality and his freedom of the will, i.e. free choice.

Even after the Fall the soul retains its capacity, helped by God's grace, to attain to the things of God and to God himself. Here lies its greatness. This capacity, this potential for union with God, is, according to Bernard, the most wonderful part of our human nature. The image can be renewed and the likeness restored so that there can be oneness of spirit and union with God.

The Image and Likeness

What have the Word and the soul in common? Much, on all counts. In the first place, there is a natural kinship, in that one is the Image of God, and the other is made in that image. Next, the resemblance argues some affinity. For the soul is made not only in the image of God but in his likeness.

Take first the Image. The Word is truth, it is wisdom and righteousness; these constitute the Image. The soul is none of these things, since it is not the Image. Yet it is capable of them and yearns for them; that perhaps is why it is said to be made in the image. It is a lofty creature, in its capacity for greatness, and in its longing we see a token of its uprightness. We read that God made man upright and great; his capacity proves that as we have said. For what is made in the image should conform to the image, and not merely share the empty name of image.

The Word is the image of this upright and great God; therefore the soul which is in his image is also like him.

The Capacity for God

Is there no difference between the Image of God and the soul which is made in its image? Indeed there is. For the soul receives according to its capacity, but the Image receives in equal measure with God. Man received his gifts from God's hands, the Image received them from God's being, that is from his very substance.

For the Image greatness is not merely the same as uprightness, but existence itself is greatness and uprightness. It is not so with the soul; its greatness and uprightness are distinct from it and from each other.

The soul is great in proportion to its capacity for the eternal, and upright in proportion to its desire for heavenly things, and the soul which does not desire or have a taste for heavenly things, but clings to earthly things, is clearly not upright but bent. But it does not for all that cease to be great, and it always retains its capacity for eternity. For even if it never attains to it, it never ceases to be capable of doing so.

And so by the greatness which it retains even when he has lost his uprightness, 'man passes as an image', but he limps as it were on one foot, and has become an estranged son.

Lord, Who is like You?

When the soul perceives this great disparity within itself, it is torn between hope and despair and can only cry, 'Lord, who is like you?' Thus the more it is offended by the evil it sees in itself, the more ardently it is drawn to the good which it likewise sees in itself, and the more it desires to become its true self, simple and righteous, fearing God and turning from evil.

But I must insist that we can only dare to undertake these things by grace, not by nature, nor even by effort. It is wisdom which overcomes malice, not effort or nature. The soul must turn to the Word. The great dignity of the soul's relationship with the Word, which I have been talking of for the past three days – is not without effect and its enduring likeness bears witness to this relationship.

The Spirit courteously admits into its fellowship one who is like him by nature. Certainly in the natural order like seeks like. He would not see the soul when she was unlike him, but when she is like him he will look upon her, and he will allow her to look upon him. 'When he will appear we shall be like him, for we shall see him as he is.' Difficult but not impossible.

The Likeness and the Vision

That likeness which accompanies the vision of God is a thing most marvellous and astonishing, and is itself the vision. I can only describe it as subsisting in charity. This vision is charity, and the likeness is charity. Who would not be amazed at the charity of God in recalling someone who has spurned him? How deserving of censure is the unrighteous man who was mentioned earlier as appropriating to himself the likeness of God, but who by choosing unrighteousness becomes incapable of loving either himself or God.

When the iniquity which is partly the cause of unrighteousness is taken away, there will be a oneness of spirit, a reciprocal vision, and reciprocal love. When what is perfect comes, what is partial will be done away with; and the love between them will be chaste and consummated, full recognition, open vision and perfect likeness. Then the soul will know as it is known and love as it is loved, and the Bridegroom will rejoice over the Bride, knowing and known, loving and loved, Jesus Christ Our Lord, who is God above all, blessed for ever. Amen.

Made in God's Image and Likeness

I believe that in these three freedoms there is contained the image and likeness of the Creator in which we were made. That in freedom of choice lies the image, and in the other two (freedom of counsel and of pleasure) is contained a certain twofold likeness. Maybe the reason why free choice alone suffers no lessening is that in it, more than in the other two, there seems to be imprinted some substantial image of the unchanging Deity.

For although free choice had a beginning, it knows no end, nor does it experience increase through righteousness, nor decrease through sin. What could be more like eternity without actually being eternity? Now in the other two freedoms, liable to diminution or even total loss, one sees a certain accidental likeness of the divine power and wisdom. By a fault we lost them; by grace we recovered them; and we can daily advance in them or fall away. They may be irreparably lost; but also securely possessed beyond the bounds of diminution. Of the likeness contained in the freedoms of counsel and pleasure nothing remains or can remain in hell. But the image remains, even there, in free choice, permanent and unchanged.

Free Choice

One point has occurred to me which I cannot neglect, and which in no way detracts from the soul's greatness and its similarity to the Word, but enhances them. This is free choice, something clearly divine which shines forth in the soul like a jewel set in gold. From it the soul derives its power of judgment, and its option of choosing between good and evil, between life and death, in fact between light and darkness.

It is the eye of the soul which as censor and arbiter exercises discrimination and discernment between these things, and arbiter in discerning and free in choosing. It is called free choice because it is exercised in these matters in accordance with the freedom of the will.

By it a person can acquire merit; everything you do, whether good or ill, which you had the choice of doing or not doing, is duly imputed to you for merit or censure. And as a person is rightly praised for refraining from doing wrong when he might have done wrong, so also someone who could have done right but did not do so, is not free from censure. But when there is no freedom there is no censure or blame.

Simplicity

Let the soul realise that by virtue of her resemblance to God, there is in her very substance a natural simplicity. This simplicity consists in the fact that for the soul it is the same thing to be as to live. But it is not the same thing to live as to live well, or to live happily. For the soul is only like to God, not equal to him. This is a degree of nearness to him, but it is only a degree.

Let us say that only for God is it the same to be as to be happy: and this is the highest and most pure simplicity. But the second is like unto this, namely that being and life should be identical. And this dignity belongs to the soul. And even though the soul belongs to this inferior degree, it can nevertheless ascend to the perfection of living well, or indeed of living in perfect happiness.

Thus the rational soul may ever glory in her resemblance to the Divinity, but still there will also ever remain between them a gulf of disparity. Still that perfection which the soul possesses is great indeed: from it, and from it alone can the ascent to the blessed life be made.

Our Unlikeness to God

The fact that Scripture speaks of our unlikeness to God does not mean that Holy Writ maintains the likeness has been destroyed, but that something different has been drawn over it, concealing it. Obviously the soul has not cast off her original form, but has put on a new one foreign to her. The latter has been added, but the former is not lost, and although that which has been superimposed has managed to obscure the natural form, it has not been able to destroy it.

'How is the gold become obscured and the finest colour changed?' cried the Prophet. He laments that the gold has lost its brightness, and that the finest colour has been obscured: but the gold is still gold, and the original base of the colour has not been wiped out. And so the simplicity of the soul remains unimpaired in its essence but it is no longer able to be seen now that it is covered over by the duplicity of man's deceit, simulation and hypocrisy.

Is it possible to find a single son of Adam who can endure to be known for what he really is? Yet, in every soul there remains the natural simplicity of man together with the duplicity that came with original sin.

5

Conversion

The wonderful opening paragraph of Sermon 83 on the Canticle tells how a person now enmeshed in sin can dare to aspire to marriage with the Word. St Bernard makes it sound so easy that some may ask if this is just theory. Does he really know what is involved? Indeed he does. His sermon on conversion given to the clerics in Paris tells us that, together with what he says about humility and our need for the help of the Word. The texts that follow form a rather unwieldy block and often overlap, but they emphasise and nuance his thought.

What he has to say is fundamental to the human situation, whether a person is living in a monastery or in the world. This may be seen more clearly in someone who has an addiction to some habit or sin. But we are all sinners, and first of all we have to acknowledge the fact. This is basic humility – truth. But it is not easy and some can never manage this first step. The admission must follow that we cannot save ourselves – from an addiction or whatever. Human power is not enough: God's help is essential. There is a further stage: we must actually ask for that help. This involves a decision to surrender one's life into the hands of the Father who cares for us, the Brother who loves us utterly, and the Spirit who heals us and gives us the power to cope or overcome. On our part, prayer and self-discipline are needed.

This whole process is so basic to human spiritual growth that the monastic life is geared to throwing us back onto God in this way. But any situation where there is no human solution can form a starting point.

Come Home Without Fear

We have seen how every soul – even if burdened with sin, enmeshed in vice, ensnared by the allurements of pleasure, a captive in exile, imprisoned in the body, caught in the mud, fixed in mire, bound to its members, a slave to care, distracted by business, afflicted with sorrow, wandering and straying, filled with anxious foreboding and uneasy suspicions, a stranger in a hostile land, and according to the prophet, sharing the defilement of the dead and counted with those who go down to hell – every soul I say, standing thus under condemnation and without hope, has the power to turn.

And then it finds it can not only breathe the fresh air of the hope of pardon and mercy, but also dare to aspire to the nuptials of the Word, not fearing to enter into alliance with God or to bear the sweet yoke of love with the King of angels.

Why should it not venture with confidence into the presence of him with whose image it sees itself honoured, and in whose likeness it knows itself made glorious? Why should it fear a majesty when its very origin gives it ground for confidence?

Conversion I

There is no true life except in conversion, and there is no other means of entering into life. 'Unless you are converted . . .' Clearly then, the conversion of souls is the working of the divine, not the human voice. May I suggest then that you prick up the ears of your heart in order to hear this inner voice and that you make an effort to hear God speaking within. That voice never ceases to knock at the door of each one of us. This voice is not only a mighty voice, but it is also a beam of light, both informing men of their transgressions and bringing to light things hidden in darkness. It opens the book of the conscience, passes in review the wretched sequence of life, unfolds its sad history, enlightens the reason, and the memory is set as it were before its own eyes.

If pride, envy, avarice, ambition or any other pest is hidden there it will scarcely be able to escape this scrutiny. If it should be guilty of any fornication, theft, cruelty, any fraud or other fault whatever the defendant will not remain hidden from this inner judge. Even though all the itching of evil pleasure quickly passes, still it stamps on the memory certain bitter marks, it leaves filthy traces.

Conversion II

If you have ever seen a man scratching at his hand and rubbing it until it bleeds, then you have a clear picture of a sinful soul. For craving gives way to suffering and mental itching yields to torment. And all the while he was scratching he was well aware that this would happen, but he pretended that it would not.

Anyone who has heard the voice of the Lord saying, 'Return transgressors, to the heart', and has discovered such foul things in his inmost chamber will set out like some detective to investigate them; he will examine each thing and search for the opening by which it filtered in. Close the windows, lock the doors, block up the openings carefully and then when fresh filth has ceased to flow, you can clean out the old.

As long as a man is without experience in the spiritual combat, he thinks that what is asked of him is easy. But the palate complains of being invited to cheap fare and denied the pleasure of getting drunk; the eyes moan that they are forbidden all titillation; the tongue says, 'I have been ordered to restrain myself from story-telling and lies'. And yet the eye is not satisfied with seeing, nor is the ear sated with hearing.

Conversion III

Now the reason sees the memory clogged with dirty things; it sees itself incapable of closing the windows thrown wide open to death; it has come to recognise its malady but finds no remedy.

Let the soul which is in this state harken to the divine voice, and to its amazement it will hear it say, 'Blessed are the poor in spirit, for theirs is the kingdom of God'. Who is poorer in spirit than the man whose spirit finds no rest? The man who is displeasing to himself is pleasing to God, and he who hates his own house, that is to say, a house full of filth and wretchedness is invited to the house of glory, a house not made with hands, eternal in the heavens. No wonder if he trembles with awe at the greatness of this honour, and says, 'Is it possible for such wretchedness to make a man happy?'

Whoever you are, if you are in this frame of mind, do not despair: it is mercy not misery that makes a man happy, but mercy's natural home is misery. Indeed misery becomes the source of man's happiness when humiliation turns into humility and necessity becomes a virtue. Sickness has real utility when it leads us into the doctor's hands, and he whom God restores to health gains by having been ill.

The Desire for Contemplation

Let such a man consider, that he will find no comfort – not within nor under nor around himself, until he at last learns to seek it from above and to hope that it will come down from above. All this will enable him to peer through the keyhole, to look through the lattices and he will discover the paradise of pleasure planted by the Lord; a flowering and lovely garden – a place of refreshment. You enter this garden not on foot, but by deeply-felt affections.

There the radiance of continence and the beholding of unblemished truth enlighten the eyes of the heart. There we have a foretaste of the incomparable delights of charity, and the spirit is pervaded with the balm of mercy and rests happily in good conscience. But these are not yet the rewards of eternal life, but only the wages paid for military service. This is the hundredfold tendered to those who scorn the world. You will consult books to no avail; you must try to experience it instead. It is wisdom, and man does not know its price. This is hidden manna, it is the new name which no one knows except him who receives it. Not learning but anointing teaches it; not science but conscience grasps it.

The Soul Wedded to the Word

So the soul returns and is converted to the Word to be re-formed by him and conformed to him. In what way? In Charity – in love. Such conformity weds the soul to the Word, for one who is like the Word by nature shows herself like him too in the exercise of her will, loving as she is loved. When she loves perfectly, the soul is wedded to the Word.

What is lovelier that this conformity? What is more desirable than charity, by whose working you approach the Word with confidence, cling to him with constancy, speak to him as a familiar friend, and refer to him in every matter with an intellectual grasp proportionate to the boldness of your desire.

Truly this is a spiritual contract, a holy marriage. It is more than a contract, it is an embrace. An embrace where identity of will makes of two, one spirit.

6

Humility

St Benedict has a very important section in his 'Rule for Monks' on humility, and Bernard preached it throughout his life. Why did he think it so important? Because humility is truth. Truth is a gift of God and it helps us to discover our identity: who we are, who we have become, and where we are going. He says: 'Be honest, take a good look at yourself, recognise yourself as you are.' This is vital, of practical value for everyone, in any walk of life. No one can do it for us. We all know the tragedy of those who refuse to do this, who refuse to admit who they are, and so they remain trapped in a world of pretence, unable to grow or move forward.

He speaks of humility of understanding which we learn from our own weaknesses and which leads to compassion for others, and also of humility of the heart which we learn only from Jesus and which leads to purity of heart. It is the pure of heart, he reminds us, who will see God.

A Deep Heart

If a man wants to know the full truth about himself he will have to get rid of the beam of pride which blocks out the light from his eye, and then set up in his heart a ladder of humility so that he can search into himself. When he has seen the truth about himself, or better when he has seen himself in truth, such a man has come to a deep heart.

Up to this he has been examining himself. Now he looks out from himself to others, exclaiming: 'Every man is a liar.' What does he mean? He means that every man is unreliable because too weak, helpless and infirm to save either himself or others.

This is very different from the conceit of the proud Pharisee. He damned all others, excepting only himself, and fooling only himself. The Psalmist shared the common mercy because he included himself in the common misery. The Pharisee waved aside mercy when he denied his misery. When in the light of Truth men know themselves, they blush at what they see. They admit that to make satisfaction is beyond their own powers, so they look beyond their own needs to the needs of their neighbours and from what they themselves have suffered, learn compassion.

Self-Knowledge

Self-knowledge is the mother of salvation, and of this mother is born humility, and the fear of the Lord which, just as it is the beginning of wisdom is the beginning of salvation. And what if you should fail to know God? How can there be any hope of salvation, where there is ignorance of God? It is impossible. For then you can neither love one whom you do know, nor possess one whom you have not loved.

Know yourself then, that you may fear God; know God that you may also love him. Knowledge of yourself will be the beginning of wisdom, knowledge of God will be the completion, the perfection of wisdom; because the fear of the Lord is the beginning of wisdom and the fulfilment of the Law is charity. Beware then, both of ignorance of yourself and ignorance of God since there is no salvation without the fear and the love of God. All other knowledge is indifferent, since the possession of it does not give us salvation.

Humility of Heart

The Saviour, when he comes, will re-form the body of our lowliness, made like to the body of his glory, only on condition, however, that he finds our hearts already re-formed and made like to the humility of his own heart. Therefore has he said, 'Learn of me, because I am meek and humble of heart.'

In connection with this I would have you notice, my Brothers, that there are two kinds of humility, the one appertaining to knowledge (or to the understanding), the other belonging to the affections (or to the will). It is this latter which Christ calls humility of the heart.

By humility of the understanding we know that we are nothing; we learn this humility from ourselves and from the experience of our own weakness. Humility of the will, or of the heart enables us to trample underfoot the glory of the world; but it is only to be learned from him who emptied himself taking the form of a servant, and who freely offered himself when they wished to make him suffer all kinds of ignominy and the shameful death of the cross . . . and who endured such torments in order to reconcile sinners to himself.

Humiliations

Although what I have written may be of no use to you, it will certainly profit my humility! While he holds his peace a fool may pass for a wise man. And so by holding my peace I could have passed for a wise man. But as it is some will laugh at my stupidity, others will mock at me as a fool, and yet others will be indignant at my presumption. All this will be of no small help to my sanctification, because humiliations lead to humility and humility is the foundation of the spiritual life.

Humiliation is the only way to humility, just as patience is the only way to peace, and reading to knowledge. If you want the virtue of humility you must not shun humiliations. If you will not suffer yourself to be humbled, you can never achieve humility. It is an advantage for me that my foolishness should be made public, that I whose lot it has often been to receive undeserved praise from those who do not know me, should now be discomforted by those who have found me out. Only the truly humble man can be said to restrain himself, sparing his own soul, because he prefers to conceal what he is, so that no one should believe him to be what he is not.

Three Degrees of Truth

There are three degrees in the perception of truth. We must look for truth in ourselves; in our neighbours; in itself. The merciful quickly grasp the truth in their neighbours when their heart goes out to them with a love that unites them so closely that they feel their neighbours' good and ill as if it were their own. Their hearts are made more clear-sighted by love, and they experience the delight of contemplating truth, not now in others but in itself.

You will never have real mercy for the failings of another until you know and realise that you have the same failings in your soul. Our Saviour has given us the example. He willed to suffer so that he might know compassion. To learn mercy he shared our misery. What in his divine nature he knows from all eternity he learned by experience in time.

I do not say he became wiser by such experience, but he was seen as being closer to us. And frail men to whom he gave the title and reality of being brothers, would have less hesitation about laying their weaknesses before him, who as God could heal them, as one close to them would heal them; and as one who had suffered the same things would understand.

Blessed are the Merciful

Anyone who asks for pardon is fittingly answered with these words: 'Blessed are the merciful, for they shall obtain mercy'. If you want God to be merciful to you, then you must be merciful towards your own soul. If you have compassion on yourself, if you struggle on in groanings of penance – for this is mercy's first step – you will arrive at mercy. If you are perhaps a frequent sinner and seek great mercy and frequent forgiveness, you must work also at increasing your mercy. Then you are reconciled to yourself, where before you had become a burden to yourself, because you had set yourself up against God.

Once peace has been restored to you in this way in your own house, the first thing to do is to extend it to your neighbours so that God may come at last to kiss you with the very kiss of his mouth. In this way being reconciled to God, as it has been written, you may have peace. Forgive those who have sinned against you, and you will be forgiven your sins when you pray to the Father with an easy conscience and say: 'Forgive us our trespasses, as we forgive those who trespass against us.'

The Taste of Wisdom

The Word is strength and he is wisdom. Let the soul draw strength from his strength and wisdom from his wisdom; let it ascribe both gifts to the Word alone. If any one has need of wisdom, let him ask it from God, who gives to all freely.

I think the same applies to virtue, for virtue is the sister of wisdom. Virtue is God's gift and must be counted among his best gifts, coming down from the Father of the Word. Virtue is characterised by strength of mind, and wisdom by peace of mind and spiritual sweetness. If any one defines wisdom as the love of virtue, I think you are not far from the truth. For where there is love there is no toil, but a taste, a savour.

Perhaps 'sapientia', that is wisdom, is derived from 'sapor', which means taste, because when it is added to virtue, like some seasoning, it adds savour to something which by itself is tasteless and bitter.

I think one could define wisdom as a taste for goodness. We lost this taste almost from the creation of our human race, when the serpent's poison infected the palate of our heart. When wisdom enters, it purifies the understanding, cleanses and heals the palate of the heart, so it tastes wisdom itself, and there is nothing better.

7

Our Need for God's Help

To know who we are, and to recognise our helplessness in the work of personal renewal is not enough. There has to be a cry from the heart to the Lord, 'I can't, you must', followed by a decision of the will to put our life in God's hands. Like the father of the Prodigal he is already running to meet us. We would not be seeking him at all unless he had first sought and loved us, unless he had nudged us, drawn us on to seek and to return home to the closest union with him.

While we were still sinners God first loved us. This is the basis not only of Bernard's Cistercian mysticism, but of Christian mysticism itself.

Renewal

Do not then, pin your hopes on ephemeral well-being, but cry to God and say: 'Do not desert me when my strength is failing.' You will ride above the vicissitudes of good and evil times with the poise of one sustained by values that are eternal, with the enduring equanimity of the man of faith who thanks God in every circumstance. Even amid the changing events and shortcomings of this world you will ensure for yourself a life of stability, provided you are renewed and reformed according to the glorious and original plan of the eternal God, the like of him in whom there is no shadow of a change.

Even in this world you will become as he is: neither dismayed by adversity nor dissolute in prosperity. Living thus, this noble creature, made to the image and likeness of his Creator, indicates that even now he is re-acquiring the dignity of that primal honour, since he deems it unworthy to be conformed to a world that is waning. Instead he strives to be re-formed by the renewal of his mind, aiming to achieve that likeness in which he knows he was created. This purpose of his compels the world itself, which was made for him to become conformed to him and co-operate for his good.

God Gives Us the Power

The soul seeks the Word, but has been first sought by the Word. Otherwise when she had gone away from the Word, or been cast out, she would not turn back to look upon the good she had left unless she were sought by the Word. For if a soul is left to herself she is like a wandering spirit which does not return. Listen to someone who was a fugitive and a wanderer: 'I have gone astray as a sheep that was lost. O seek your servant.'

Do you want to return? But if it is a matter of your own will, why do you ask for help? Clearly because one cannot do it alone. If a soul desires to return and asks to be sought, whence does it obtain this desire? If I am not mistaken, it is the result of the soul being already sought and visited by God. And his seeking has not been fruitless, because it has activated the will, without which there could be no return.

But the soul is so feeble and the return so difficult, that it is not enough to be sought only once. The soul may have the will to return, but the will cannot act unless it has some supporting power. So the psalmist prays, 'O seek your servant'; he is asking that the God who had given him the will to seek, might also give him the power to do so.

The Search for God

The soul rises and goes about the city, and seeks her beloved through the streets and squares. Let her seek him as she can provided she remembers that she was first sought, just as she was first loved.

It is because of this that she herself both seeks and loves. Let us also pray, brethren, that his mercies may go before us, for our need is great. 'I sought him whom my soul loves' – this is what you are urged to do by the goodness of him who awaits you, and loved you before you loved him. You would not seek him or love him unless you had first been sought and loved.

Not only in one blessing have you been forestalled but in two, being loved as well as being sought. For the love is the reason for the search, and the search is the fruit of the love, and its certain proof.

You are loved, so do not suppose you are sought to be punished. You are sought so that you may not complain you are loved in vain. Both these loving favours should give you courage, and drive away your diffidence, persuading you to return, and stirring your affections. From this comes the zeal to seek him whom your soul loves, because you cannot seek unless you are sought, and when you are sought you cannot but seek.

Returning to God

Do you have the effrontery, the insolence, to return to him whom you spurned in your arrogance? It will be a wonder if you do not meet the judge rather than the bridegroom.

'I do not fear, because I love; and I could not love at all if I were not loved.' One who is loved has nothing to fear. Let those fear who do not love. Since I love, I cannot doubt that I am loved, any more that I can doubt that I love. Nor can I fear to look upon his face, since I have sensed his tenderness.

In what way? In this – not only has he sought me as I am, but he has shown me tenderness, and caused me to seek him with confidence. How can he be angry with me for seeking him, when he overlooked the contempt I showed for him? He will not drive away someone who seeks him, when he actually sought someone who spurned him.

The spirit of the Word is gentle, he searches the deep things of God, and knows his thoughts – thoughts of peace and not of vengeance. How can I fail to be inspired to seek him, when I have experienced his mercy and been assured of his peace? Brothers, to realise this is to be taught by the Word; to be convinced of it is to be found.

The Goodness of God

If this horrible fear should ever besiege your heart, silently suggesting that your worship of God is not acceptable and that your repentance is fruitless because you cannot correct the matter in which you have offended him, do not for one moment give way to it, but answer it faithfully by saying to yourself: I have done evil, but it is done and cannot be undone. Who can tell whether God has not foreseen that it would profit me, that he who is good has not wished that good should accrue to me out of the evil I have done? May he punish me for what I have done amiss, but let the good he has provided for me remain.

The goodness of God knows how to use our disordered wishes and actions, often lovingly turning them to our advantage. What loving care the divine goodness has for us! Never does it cease to pour forth its blessings, not only where it can see nothing to deserve them, but often where it sees everything to the contrary!

I wish you to fear in order that you may repent. Not to fear, so that you may presume. To presume so that you do not lose heart. Not to presume so that you become slothful.

To be Re-formed by the Word

There is a great natural gift within us, and if it is not allowed full play the rest of our nature will go to ruin, as though it were being eaten away by the rust of decay. This would be an insult to its Creator. This is why God, its Creator, desires the divine glory and nobility to be always preserved in the soul, so that it may have within itself that by which it may always be admonished by the Word, either to stay with him or to return to him if it has strayed.

It does not stray by changing its place or by walking, but it strays in its affections or rather in its defections, and it becomes unlike itself when it becomes unlike him through its way of life. But this unlikeness is not the destruction of its nature but a defect, for natural goodness is increased as much by comparison with itself as it is spoiled by communication with evil.

So the soul returns and is converted to the Word to be re-formed by him and conformed to him. In what way? In charity – For he says, 'Be imitators of God, like dear children and walk in love, as Christ also has loved you.'

The Help of the Word

'Who shall climb the mountain of the Lord?' If anyone aspires to reach the summit of that mountain, the perfection of virtue, he will know how hard the climb is, and how the attempt is doomed to failure without the help of the Word. Unless it leans on him, its struggle is in vain. But it will gain strength by struggling with itself and, becoming stronger, will impel all things towards reason: anger, fear, covetousness, and joy. Like a good driver, it will control the vehicle of the mind, bringing every carnal affection, and every sense under the control of reason in accordance with virtue.

Surely all things are possible to someone who leans upon him who can do all things? What confidence there is in the cry, 'I can do all things in him who strengthens me!' Nothing shows more clearly the almighty power of the Word than that he makes all-powerful all those who put their hope in him. For all things are possible to one who believes.

So, I say, neither power, nor treachery, nor lure, can overthrow or hold in subjection the mind which rests upon the Word and is clothed with strength from above.

The Bride of the Word

The soul which has attained this degree of likeness to the Word now ventures to think of marriage. Why should she not, when she sees that she is like him and therefore ready for marriage? His loftiness has no terrors for her, because her likeness to him associates her with him, and her declaration of love is a betrothal. This is the form of that declaration: 'I have sworn and I purpose to keep your righteous judgments.' The Apostles followed this when they said, 'See we have left everything to follow you.'

When you see a soul leaving everything and clinging to the Word with all her will and desire, living for the Word, ruling her life by the Word, conceiving what the Word will bring forth by her, so that she can say, 'For me to live is Christ and to die is gain,' you know that the soul is the spouse and bride of the Word.

The heart of the Bridegroom has faith in her, knowing her to be faithful, for she has rejected all things as dross to gain him.

8

Finding God in the Church

Bernard was a Churchman – a man of the Church – in the very best sense of the word. For him, the Bride of the Canticle was primarily the Church. He speaks beautifully of the seamless robe of unity which Christ left to his Church, and he worked tirelessly to preserve this unity. He said that as members of the Church we share in her special relationship with Christ, and it is in the Church and through her liturgical feasts and sacraments that we enter into the mysteries of Christ's earthly life, and share in their redemptive power.

As Abbot, Bernard preached on all the great feasts. His sermons were scriptural and practical, and often mnemonic to help the Brothers when they went out to work. He tried to show the particular graces each feast had for the Brothers, and how they could make them their own. We must remember, of course, that he was speaking and writing in the context of a twelfth century monastic culture.

Especially noteworthy are the little blocks of sermons for Advent and Christmas (for which he had a special attraction), and those to do with the Paschal Mystery. He also made his own the 'little bundle of Myrrh' of the Canticle and is often portrayed with his arms full of the instruments of the Passion.

The Church

Which of us can live uprightly and perfectly even for one hour? Yet there is one who can truthfully glory in this praise. She is the Church, whose fulness is a never-ceasing fount of intoxicating joy, perpetually fragrant. For what she lacks in one member she possesses in another according to the measure of Christ's gift and the plan of the Spirit who distributes to each one just as he chooses. With bold assurance she lays claim to the title of bride. And although none of us will dare to arrogate for his own soul the title of bride of the Lord, nevertheless we are members of the Church which rightly boasts of this title, and so we may justifiably assume a share in this honour. For what all of us simultaneously possess in a full and perfect manner, that, each single one of us undoubtedly possesses by partcipation.

Thank you Lord Jesus, for your kindness in uniting us to the Church you so dearly love, not merely that we may be endowed with the gift of faith, but that like brides we may be one with you in an embrace that is sweet, chaste and eternal, beholding with unveiled faces that glory which is yours in union with the Father and the Holy Spirit for ever and ever, Amen.

The Robe of Christ

To his Bride, the Church, Christ left his own robe, a many coloured robe, woven from top to bottom. It is many-coloured because of the many different Orders distinguished within it. It is seamless because of the undivided unity of a love that cannot be torn apart, as it is written: 'Who will separate us from the love of Christ?'

Therefore let there be no division within the Church. Let it remain whole and entire according to its inherited right. Concerning the Church it has been written: 'At your right hand stands the queen in a golden robe, embroidered with varying patterns.'

This is why different people receive different gifts. One person is allotted one kind of gift, one another, irrespective of whether they be a Cistercian or a Cluniac, a Regular or one of the laity. This applies to every order and to all languages, to both sexes, to every age and condition of life, everywhere and always, from the first person down to the last.

The Robe of Unity

Therefore let us all work together to form a single robe, and let this robe include us all. It is not I by myself, nor you without me, nor a third person on his own, who can form this one robe, but all of us together, provided we take care to maintain the unity of the Spirit in the bond of peace. I repeat, it is not our Order alone, nor yours alone that makes up this unity, but ours and yours together.

Why wonder at this variety during the time of exile, while the Church is on pilgrimage? Why wonder that its unity is also plurality? Just as there are many rooms in a single house, so there are many different Orders in the one Church. . . . Unity consists in the singleness of love.

There are many paths which can be taken, for the dwelling places to which we journey are many. Whatever path a person is taking, let them not be so concerned about alternative routes that they lose sight of their destination.

Let them be sure that by following the path they are on, they will eventually arrive at one of the dwelling places, and so will not be left outside their Father's house.

The Lord Jesus

I would like to begin with a word from St Paul: 'If anyone does not love the Lord Jesus, let him be anathema.' Truly, I ought to love the one through whom I have my being, my life, my understanding. If I am ungrateful, I am unworthy too. 'Lord Jesus, whoever refuses to live for you is clearly worthy of death, and is in fact dead already. Whoever does not know you is a fool. And whoever wants to become something without you, without doubt that person is considered nothing and is just that. O God, whoever wants to live for himself and not for you, in all that he does is nothing.'

The love of Jesus was sweet, and wise, and strong. I call it sweet because he took on a human body, wise because he avoided sin, strong because he endured death. Even though he took a body his love was never sensual, but always in the wisdom of the Spirit. How sweet it is to see as man the Creator of humanity. A dear friend, a wise counsellor, a strong helper. Should I not willingly entrust myself to the one who had the good will, the wisdom, the strength to save me? He sought me out, he called me through grace; will he refuse me as I come to him?

Human Affection for Christ

Notice that the love of the heart is, in a certain sense, carnal, because our hearts are attracted most towards the humanity of Christ and the things he did or commanded while in the flesh. The heart that is filled with this love is quickly touched by every word on this subject.

The soul at prayer should have before it a sacred image of the God-Man, in his birth or infancy or as he was teaching, or dying, or rising again, or ascending. Whatever form it takes this image must bind the soul with the love of virtue and expel vices, eliminate temptations and quieten desires. I think this is the principal reason why the invisible God willed to be seen in the flesh and to converse with men as a man. He wanted to recapture the affections of carnal men who were unable to love in any other way, by first drawing them to the saving love of his own humanity, and then gradually to raise them to a spiritual love.

It was only by love of his physical presence that they had left everything. Afterwards he showed them a higher degree of love when he said, 'It is the Spirit who gives life, the flesh profits nothing.'

God's Self-emptying

That self-emptying was neither a simple gesture nor a limited one. He emptied himself even to the assuming of human nature, even to accepting death, death on a cross. Who is there that can adequately gauge the greatness of the humility, gentleness, and self-surrender, revealed by the Lord of majesty in assuming human nature, and in accepting the punishment of death, with the shame of the cross? But somebody will say: 'Surely the Creator could have restored his original plan without all that hardship?'

Yes, he could, but he chose the way of personal suffering so that we would never again have a reason to display that worst and most hateful of all vices, ingratitude. If his decision did involve painful weariness for himself, it was meant also to involve us in a debt that only great love can repay.

He who was Lord became a slave, he who was rich became a pauper, the Word was made flesh, and the Son of God did not disdain to become the son of man. So may it please you to remember that, even if you are made out of nothing, you have not been redeemed out of nothing.

The Three Unions

In assuming our flesh the majesty of God by an exercise of omnipotence effected three unions, wonderfully unique. For the Divine Nature was united to human nature, virginity to motherhood, and faith to the heart of man.

The Divine and Sovereign Trinity has shown us the most wonderful thing in creation: the Word, the soul, and human flesh are united in the unity of a single person. So, remember, that you are dust and do not be proud; remember also that you are made one with God and be not ungrateful.

According to the ordinary course of nature, virginity is never found co-existent with fecundity, nor is there any room for fecundity where virginity is preserved intact. Mary is the only woman in whom integrity and motherhood have met together. In her was once accomplished what had never been done before nor shall be done again.

It is very extraordinary how the heart of man gives assent to these two mysteries. Just as iron and clay cannot be welded together, so it is impossible to join so mighty a force of faith with the inconstancy of the human heart, without the solder of the Holy Spirit.

Reconciliation

To us a Child is given indeed, but in him dwells the fulness of the Godhead. For when the fulness of time was come, the fulness of the Godhead came also. . . . What is there that so builds up faith strengthens our hope, and kindles our charity as the humanity of God? . . . For what have I to fear when the Saviour comes to my house?

He is a little Child and easily appeased. See, is he not made very little for our sakes, and can we not be reconciled for very little? For very little, mind you, but not without repentance because our penitence is a very little thing. We are poor and have little to give; but we can be forgiven for that little, if we will. This miserable body is all I have to give; but if I give that, it will be enough, provided that I add his body to my own, for that is of mine and belongs to me.

From you O Lord, I beg that which I have not in myself. Sweet and easy is this reconciliation, small is the satisfaction that I am required to make; but it must not be reckoned as of small account. For now it is made easily, later it will be hard. Now there is no one who cannot be reconciled; but later on there will be nobody who can.

9

The Lord Jesus

We have placed a number of texts on the person of Christ among those in the Liturgical Year, for we cannot really separate our personal devotion to Christ and his place in the Liturgy. 'Write what you will, I shall not relish it unless it tells of Jesus': this is the mind of Bernard and we are very close to his heart when we read what he has to say about the name of Jesus and its healing power.

The sufferings of Christ had a large place in Bernard's devotion: the 'little bundle of myrrh' as he referred to them. If he had a motto it was, 'My beloved is to me a little bundle of myrrh'. He had it written on a rough piece of wood which he hung in his cell, and which was later buried with him.

He was familiar with the heart of 'My Lord Jesus', overflowing with mercy, to which he went with all confidence. When he felt tired and arid, he turned to the companionship of Jesus who did not fail to drive away all his feelings of tension and weariness.

It is in these texts especially, that we meet Bernard the man and the monk. A simple person sitting with the Lord in the house of Martha and Mary; the fire and the energy are quietened, he is at our side yet so much 'deeper in'.

Like St Teresa, he tells us we can never have done with meditating on the God-Man, we can never outgrow gazing on the human face of Christ, for he is the way to the Father. But Christ has ascended, and Bernard leads us on to a higher degree of love, to union with the Word in Christ whom we contact through faith in spirit and in truth.

The Name of Jesus

The name of Jesus is more than light, it is also food. Do you not feel increase of strength as often as you remember it? What other name can so enrich the man who meditates? What can equal its power to refresh the harassed senses, to buttress the virtues, to add vigour to good and upright habits, to foster chaste affections?

Every food of the mind is dry if it is not dipped in that oil; it is tasteless if not seasoned by that salt. Write what you will, I shall not relish it unless it tells of Jesus. Talk or argue about what you will, I shall not relish it if you exclude the name of Jesus. Jesus to me is honey in the mouth, music in the ear, a song in the heart.

Again it is a medicine. Does one of us feel sad? Let the name of Jesus come into his heart, from there let it spring to his mouth, so that shining like the dawn it may dispel all darkness and make a cloudless sky. Does someone fall into sin? Does his despair even urge him to suicide? Let him but invoke this lifegiving name and his will to live will be at once renewed.

And where is the man, who terrified and trembling before impending peril, has not suddenly been filled with courage and rid of fear by calling on the strength of that name?

The Healing Power of the Name of Jesus

Where is the man who, tossed on the rolling seas of doubt did not quickly find certitude by recourse to the power of the name of Jesus? Was ever a man so discouraged, so beaten down by afflictions, to whom the sound of his name did not bring new resolve? In short, for all the ills and disorders to which the flesh is heir, this name is medicine.

Nothing so curbs the onset of anger, controls unbridled extravagance and quenches the flame of lust; it cools the thirst of covetousness and banishes the itch of unclean desire. For when I name Jesus I set before me a man who is meek and humble of heart, kind, prudent, chaste, merciful, flawlessly upright and holy in the eyes of all.

And this same man is the all-powerful God whose way of life heals me, whose support is my strength. Because he is a man I strive to imitate him; because of his divine power I lean upon him. The examples of his human life I gather like medicinal herbs; with the aid of his power I blend them, and the result is a compound such as no pharmacist can produce.

I Am the Way

'I am the Way, the Truth, and the Life.' The way is humility, the goal is truth. The first is the labour, the second is the reward. But you may ask: 'How do I know that Our Lord is speaking of humility? He only uses a general word, "I am the Way" '? Well, I will give you a clearer test. 'Learn of me for I am meek and humble of heart.' He points to himself as an example of humility, a model of meekness.

Imitate him and you will not walk in darkness but will have the light of life. What is the light of life but truth that enlightens every man that comes into this world and shows us where the true life is to be found?

So, when he says: 'I am the Way and the Truth', he adds, 'and the Life'. It is as if he said: 'I am the Way, I lead to Truth: I am the Truth, I promise Life; and I myself am the very life I give you.' 'For this is eternal life, that they may know you the one true God and Jesus Christ whom you have sent.'

Supposing, then you go on to object: 'I see the way – humility; I long for the goal to which it leads – truth; but what if the way is so difficult that I can never reach the goal?' The answer comes promptly: 'I am the Life', that is, I am the food, the viaticum, to sustain you on your journey.

Christ Feeds Us and is Fed by Us

In the days of his earthly life Christ ate at the house of Martha and Mary, and refreshed his spirit with their devotion and virtues. But I think he was giving them a food of a spiritual kind. He fed them in the same way as he himself was fed. So it is that while he feeds others he is himself fed, and while he refreshes us with spiritual joy he himself rejoices in our spiritual progress.

My penitence, my salvation, are his food. I myself am his food. I am chewed as I am reproved by him; I am swallowed by him as I am taught; I am digested by him as I am changed; I am assimilated as I am transformed; I am made one with him as I am conformed to him.

He feeds upon us and is fed by us that we may be the more closely bound to him. Otherwise we are not perfectly united with him. He eats me that he may have me in himself, and he in turn is eaten by me that he may be in me, and the bond between us will be strong and the union complete. For I shall be in him and he will likewise be in me.

Lent with the Church

Today, dear brethren, we enter the holy season of Lent, our Christian period of military service. In keeping it, we do not stand alone. We are united with all who hold the faith. Should not all Christians share the fast of Christ? Where the Head leads, should not the members follow? If from the Head we have received good things, shall we not also receive painful things? Would we refuse the sorrowful, yet share the pleasant? If so we prove ourselves unworthy to be joined to him; for everything he suffers is for us. It is no great thing, surely for a man to fast with Christ, when he hopes to sit with him at his Father's table. Nor is it much for the member to suffer with the Head, seeing he stands to share his glory too.

Happy the member who clings to the Head through all, and follows him wherever he goes; for otherwise, if he be parted from him, he will lose the spirit of life.

Lord you carry my griefs and grieve for my sake; and through the narrow door of the passion, you enter first, to make a wider passage for your members that follow you.

The Palm Sunday Procession

I want you to see in this procession, dearest brethren, an image of the glory of our heavenly fatherland, and in the Passion the way that leads to it. For the trials of this present time are the way to life, the way to glory, the way to the holy city, the way to the kingdom of God according to the witness of the thief who said from his cross 'Lord remember me when you come into your kingdom.'

The thief beheld Christ on his way to his kingdom, and begged to be remembered by him when he arrived there. He also came there as a result of his prayer; and by how short a journey you may gather from the fact that he was deemed worthy to be with the Lord in Paradise on that very day.

Thus the glory of the procession renders the pains of the Passion easy to endure, because nothing appears difficult to the soul that loves.

The Sufferings of Christ

'My beloved is to me a little bundle of myrrh.' From the early days of my conversion, conscious of my grave lack of merits, I made sure to gather for myself this little bundle of myrrh. It was culled from all the anxious hours and bitter experiences of my Lord. First from the privations of his infancy, then from the hardships he endured in preaching, the fatigues of his journeys, the long watches in prayer, the temptations when he fasted, his tears of compassion, the heckling when he addressed the people, and finally the dangers from traitors in the brotherhood.

There were the insults, the spitting, the blows, the mockery, the scorn, the nails and similar torments, and all for the salvation of our race. Among the little branches of this perfumed myrrh I feel we must not forget the myrrh which he drank upon the cross and was used for his anointing at his burial. In the first of these he took upon himself the bitterness of my sins, in the second he affirmed the future incorruption of my body. As long as I live I shall proclaim the abounding goodness in these events; for all eternity I shall not forget these mercies, for in them I have found life.

The Wounds of Christ

Someone expounding this passage, 'my dove in the clefts of the rock', interpreted 'the clefts of the rock' to mean the wounds of Christ, which I entirely approve of, since 'Christ is the rock'. What can be found in the Rock except what is most excellent? It makes me feel secure, it gives me a firm footing.

On the Rock I am safe from my enemies. And where shall the weak find a safe rest or a secure refuge except in the wounds of the Saviour. I have sinned most grievously but I am not confounded because I will call to mind the wounds of my Saviour. For he was wounded for our sins. What sin can be so much 'unto death' as that it cannot be 'loosed' by the death of Christ? Therefore no disease however desperate, shall have power to drive me to despair, if only I keep in mind so powerful and effective a remedy.

Brethren, whatever I see to be wanting in me, I appropriate for myself with all confidence from the heart of my Lord Jesus. For his heart overflows with mercy, neither does it lack clefts for the outpouring of its treasures. They pierced his hands and his feet and opened his side with a lance. And through these clefts I am allowed to 'suck honey from the rock and oil from the hardest stone'.

Resurrection

Resurrection is passing over, passing on. Christ did not come back, he passed over. He did not return, he passed on. The very name Pasch means 'pass over', not 'come back'; and Galilee means 'passing on', and not 'return'. If, after his death on the cross, the Lord Christ had lived again under the conditions of our mortality amid all the troubles of this present life, I should have said not that he had passed over but that he had come back. But because he has in fact passed over into newness of life, he invites us also to pass over.

Shall we deprive the Resurrection of its name of Pasch by making it an opportunity of going back, rather than of passing over? Shall we be found as meddlesome, as talkative, as lazy and as careless as we were before? Are people going to find us conceited again and suspicious, backbiters and bad tempered, and enmeshed in all the vices that we have deplored these days (of Lent) with such solicitude? This is not passing on, my brothers, not so will you see Christ, for this is not the way by which God shows us his salvation.

Passing Beyond

The Lord Jesus passed not only from death to life, but passed beyond to glory. If he had indeed risen from the dead but had not ascended into heaven, one could only say that he had passed by, not that he had passed beyond to glory, and that the Bride who seeks him must only pass by and need not pass beyond. But since he had passed by in his Resurrection and had passed beyond in his Ascension, she too had to pass beyond in faith and devotion and follow him even to heaven. To believe in the Resurrection, is to pass by, but to believe in the Ascension is to pass beyond.

Christ is the first fruits – he has gone before and our faith has gone with him. Where would it not follow him? If he goes up to heaven our faith is there; if he goes down to hell it is there. If he takes the wings of the morning and dwells in the uttermost parts of the sea, even there his hand will lead me, and his right hand hold me. Is it not then through our faith that the omnipotent and good God has raised us and made us sit down at his right hand?

Thus the Church said, 'I left them behind', for she has left herself behind, abiding in faith where she had not yet come in fact.

Christ our Companion

When men grow weary of studying spiritual doctrine and become lukewarm, when their spiritual energies are drained away, then they walk in sadness along the ways of the Lord. They fulfil the tasks enjoined on them with hearts that are tired and arid, they grumble without ceasing. If when we are subject to these moods, the compassionate Lord draws near to us on the way, and being from heaven begins to talk to us about heavenly truths, sings our favourite air from among the songs of Zion, speaks about the city of God and its peace, and on the life that is eternal, I assure this happy talk will drive away all tension from the hearer's mind and weariness from his body.

For our meditations on the Word who is the Bridegroom, on his glory, his elegance, power and majesty, become in a sense his way of speaking to us. When with eager minds we examine his rulings, when we meditate on his law day and night, let us be assured that the Bridegroom is present, and that he speaks his message of happiness to us lest our trials should prove more than we can bear. Beware of seeing these thoughts as your own, rather acknowledge that he is present.

The Gift of the Spirit

No one who loves God need have any doubt that God loves him. God gladly returns our love, which was preceded by his own. How could he be reluctant to love us in response to our love for him, when he already loved us before ever we loved him at all? Yes, I say, God loved us. We have a pledge of his love in the Spirit and a faithful witness to it in Jesus – a double and irrefutable proof of the love God bears towards each one of us. Christ died for us, and so deserves our love.

The Spirit moves us by his grace and so enables us to love. Christ gives us the reason, the Spirit gives us the power. The one sets before us the example of his own great love, the other gives us the love itself.

In Christ we see the object of our love, by the Spirit we are empowered to love him. We can say then that the former supplies the motive for charity, the latter the volition. How shameful it would be to see God's Son dying for us without being moved to gratitude! Yet this could easily happen if the Spirit were lacking.

The love of God has been poured into our hearts by the Holy Spirit he has given us, and so we love him in return for his love, and by loving him we deserve to be loved still more.

Faith

The Apostle tells us that Christ dwells in our hearts by faith. We may take that as meaning that Christ lives in us as long as faith does. When faith dies, however, then in a sense Christ also dies in us. And faith is dead when it lacks works; our works bear witness to our faith's vitality, just as the movements of the body show that the body lives. And the life of faith is charity, as the Apostle says, 'Faith works by love'; and charity is spread abroad in our hearts by the Holy Spirit.

Therefore when charity grows cold, faith dies, just as the body dies when the soul departs from it. So if you see a person active in good works and joyful in the zest of living, you know from these indubitable proofs that faith is alive in them.

Just as the flower by necessity precedes the fruit, so faith ought to come before good works. Without faith it is impossible to please God. Hence there is neither fruit without a flower nor a good work without faith. So the mind accustomed to quietude receives consolation from good works rooted in sincere faith.

St Peter and St Paul

My brothers, the pastors and teachers appointed for men ought to have meekness, power and wisdom. They ought to be meek, that they may receive me with kindness and compassion; they ought to be powerful, to afford me a secure protection; they ought to be wise, in order that they may bring me to the path and along the path that leads to the holy city.

Now where can you find greater meekness than that shown by Peter . . . who invited all sinners to come to him? Where greater power than that of him to whom the very earth was obedient, giving up the dead at his command? Where will you find greater wisdom than his, to whom not flesh and blood but the Father in heaven communicated with such generosity that wisdom which comes down from heaven?

What have the holy apostles taught us, and what are they teaching us still? Not the art of fishing, or tent-making, nor anything of that kind; not how to read Plato, or how to be always learning and never arriving at the knowledge of the Truth.

No, what Peter and Paul have taught me is how I ought to live.

The Pharisee and the Publican

Consider now that Pharisee who prayed in the Temple. He was not an extortioner, he was not unjust, neither was he an adulterer. He fasted twice in the week and gave tithes of all he possessed. You are now perhaps thinking he was ungrateful? But hear what he said: 'O God I give you thanks that I am not like the rest of men . . .'. No, the obstacle to grace in him was that his heart was not free from self-righteousness, it was not emptied out, it was not humble but rather proud and elated. For instead of trying to discover what was yet wanting in himself, he exaggerated his merits. Therefore, he who imagined himself to be full went down to his house empty.

The Publican, on the contrary, did in truth empty himself; and because he took care to bring his vessel empty, he returned with a bountiful outpouring of grace.

Therefore, dear brothers, if we too wish to find grace, let us not only avoid sin in the future, but also do worthy penance for the sins of the past, and be careful to prove ourselves devoted to God and sincerely humble.

The Holy Angels

Consider, dearest brethren, how careful we ought to be to show ourselves worthy of such noble company and so to live in the sight of the holy angels that they shall see nothing in our conduct to displease them. For woe to us if ever it should happen that provoked by our sins and indifference, they deem us undeserving of their visits and their company.

Then in truth, we shall be obliged to lament, because those had withdrawn who could have protected me by their presence and driven off my enemies. If, then, we find the companionship of the angels so necessary for us, we ought carefully to avoid anything that could displease them and to cultivate those virtues especially in which they take particular delight. Now there are many things which afford them pleasure and which they are glad to find in us, such as sobriety, chastity, voluntary poverty, frequent ejaculations to God, prayers offered up with contrite tears and a pure intention of the heart.

But above and beyond all these, unity and peace the 'angels of Peace' demand from us. We ought to think and speak alike and have no divisions amongst us, but rather to show that we are all, collectively, one body in Christ and members individually one of another.

Guardian Angels

He has given his Angels charge of you to guard you in all your ways. How this ought to produce respect in you, to promote devotion and to provide confidence! Respect because of the presence of the Angels, devotion because of their friendliness, and confidence because of their guardianship. His Angels are everywhere, in every nook and cranny respect your Angel. They are present not only with you, but even for you. To protect you and to benefit you. What shall you repay to the Lord for all he has given you?

What have we to fear under such guardians? Those who guard us in all our ways cannot be overcome or led astray, or much less lead us astray. They are faithful, they are prudent, they are powerful. What should we fear? Let us simply follow them, stay close to them, and we shall dwell in the protection of the God of heaven. Each time you feel some great temptation, and strong tribulation pressing in, call on your guardian, your guide, who is your helper in tribulation. Call upon him, he does not sleep, nor does he slumber. Be familiar with the Angels, Brothers, visit them often by careful meditation and devout prayer, for they are always near to comfort and protect you.

The Cross

St Andrew threatened by the torture of the cross answered: 'If I had feared the cross, I should not have proclaimed its glory.' Then seeing it prepared, he cried, 'Hail precious cross, that received honour and beauty from the limbs of the Lord! Hail, cross that was hallowed by the body of Christ and by his limbs was enriched as with pearls.'

When we were singing these words of Andrew at Matins last night, did none of us say to himself, 'What is the sense of it? Is the cross really precious? Is it a thing that can be loved? Is it a thing of joy?'

Yes, brothers, it is. The tree of the cross bears the bud of life . . . it is a fruitful, a health-giving tree. How should it otherwise have occupied that Ground, or how should its nail-roots have pierced that supremely precious Soil? It would never have been planted in that Garden, never have been allowed to occupy that Vineyard, had it not been more precious and more fruitful than any other tree.

10

The Cistercian Way of Life

Bernard had heard the word of Jesus, 'Follow me'. For him it was to be by way of the monastic/Cistercian life; there was never to be any other way. And he drew many to follow Christ at Clairvaux, which he regarded, like the Church, as an earthly Jerusalem linked to the Holy City in heaven. In spite of his absences on the business of the Church his heart was rooted at Clairvaux – he was always a monk and thought as a monk. The monastic yoke of Christ was a light burden which even carried those on whom it was laid. It was a service of joy and gladness, which could not be explained in words or learnt in books: the knowledge came from experience.

Bernard was an excellent psychologist, aware of all the twists and turns of human nature, and through a deep self-knowledge and knowledge of others, he became a compassionate and merciful guide for his monks. He understood thoroughly that in the struggle with our faults and failings, we need more than our own human resources. Our good works are done not only for God, but by God working in partnership with us.

The Cistercian Way

Our way of life is an awareness of our need. It is humility, it is poverty freely accepted, obedience, and joy in the Holy Spirit. Our way of life means learning to be silent, exerting ourselves in fasts, vigils, prayers. It means working with our hands, and above all clinging to that most excellent way which is love. It means furthermore to advance day by day in these things, and to persevere in them.

I trust that this is what you are busily doing. There is one thing you have done at which everyone marvels. It is that, although your lives were holy, you thought nothing of this but made it your business to share the holy lives of others that yours might become yet more holy. It is so rare that anyone leading a good life is ready to do this, that when it happens everyone admires it.

The Cistercian family welcomed you with open arms, and the angels looked down upon you with smiling faces. They know very well that what pleases God more than anything is brotherly concord and unity, since the prophet says: 'Gracious is the sight and full of comfort, when brothers dwell together in unity'; and again: 'When brother helps brother, theirs is the strength of a fortress.'

Monastic Life: a Second Baptism

You have also asked my opinion on monastic profession considered as a second baptism. Why has our way of life rather than other penitential callings merited to be called this? I think it is because of the more perfect renouncement of the world and the special excellence of such a spiritual way of life. For it restores the divine image in the soul and makes us Christ-like, much as baptism does. It is also like another baptism in that we mortify the earthly side of our nature, so that we may be more and more clothed with Christ, being thus again 'buried in the likeness of his death'. Just as in baptism we are delivered from the power of darkness and carried over into the kingdom of light, so likewise in the second regeneration of this holy profession we are refashioned in the light of virtue, being delivered, not now from the unique darkness of original sin, but from many actual sins.

To the Parents of a Novice

If God is making your son his own, as well as yours, so that he may become even richer, even more noble, even more distinguished and, what is better than all this, so that from being a sinner he may become a saint, what do either you or he lose? But he must prepare himself for the kingdom which has been prepared for him from the beginning of the world . . .

Knowing that he is tender and delicate perhaps you are afraid for his health under the harshness of our life. . . . Have comfort, do not worry, I shall look after him like a father and he will be to me a son until the Father of mercies, the God of all consolation, shall receive him from my hands. Do not be sad about your Geoffrey or shed any tears on his account, for he is going quickly to joy and not to sorrow.

I will be for him both a mother and a father, both a brother and a sister. I will make the crooked path straight for him and the rough places smooth. I will temper and arrange all things that his soul may advance and his body not suffer. He will serve the Lord with joy and gladness, 'his song will be of the Lord's, for great is the glory of the Lord'.

Christ's Yoke is Easy

It is pleasant to admire the lightness of the burden of Truth. And indeed it is really light for not only is it no burden for the man who carries it, but it even carries him! And what can be lighter than a burden which not only does not burden, but even carries him on whom it is laid?

This is the burden which the Virgin bore and by which she was borne and not burdened. This is the burden which supported the very arms of the old Simeon who bore it in his arms. And this is what snatched Paul up to the third heaven, even when he was weighed down by the corruptible body.

When I look for an example to illustrate this disburdening burden, nothing occurs to me more apt than the wings of a bird, for they, in an extraordinary way render the body both greater and yet more nimble. What a wonderful thing that a body should be made lighter by its very increase in size, so that the more it increases in bulk the more it decreases in weight. Here we have a clear illustration of the sweet burden of Christ which carries those who carry it.

To Henry Murdac

What wonder if you are tossed about between prosperity and adversity since you have not yet gained a foothold on the rock. Oh, if only you knew, if only I could explain to you! If you could but taste for a moment the full ears of corn on which Jerusalem feasts.

If I could but have you as my fellow in the school of piety of which Jesus is the master! How gladly would I share with you the warm loaves which, still piping hot, fresh, as it were, from the oven, Christ of his heavenly bounty so often breaks with his poor!

Believe me who have experience, you will find much more when labouring among woods than you ever will amongst books. Woods and stones will teach you what you can never hear from any master. Do you imagine you cannot suck honey from the rocks and oil from the hardest stone; that the mountains do not drop sweetness and the hills flow with milk and honey; that the valleys are not filled with corn? So many things occur to me that I cannot restrain myself. But as it is for prayers and not a sermon that you have asked me, I will pray God that he may open your heart. Farewell.

Clairvaux

I write to tell you that your Philip has found a short cut to Jerusalem. Even now he stands in the courts of Jerusalem. He has entered the holy city and has chosen his heritage with them of whom it has been said: 'You are no longer exiles or aliens; the saints are your fellow citizens, you belong to God's household.' His going and coming is in their company and he has become one of them, glorifying God and saying with them: 'We find our true home in heaven'. He is no longer an inquisitive onlooker, but a devout inhabitant and an enrolled citizen of Jerusalem; not of that earthly Jerusalem to which Mount Sinai in Arabia is joined, but of that free Jerusalem which is above and is the mother of us all.

And this if you want to know, is Clairvaux. She is the Jerusalem united to the one in heaven by wholehearted devotion, by conformity of life, and by a certain spiritual affinity. Here, Philip promises himself, will be his rest for ever and ever. He has chosen to dwell here because he has found, not yet, the fulness of vision, but certainly the hope of that true peace, 'the peace of God which surpasses all our understanding'.

To Aelred of Rievaulx

I have besought you, I have commanded you to write some little thing for me. You have said that you are ignorant of grammar, that you have come to the desert not from the schools but from the kitchen. That you have since, lived a rustic and rough life amidst rock and mountains, earning in the sweat of your brow your daily bread with axe and maul; and that flights of oratory ill become your poor fisherman's clothes. I most gratefully accept your excuses, because knowledge that comes from the school of the Holy Spirit rather than the schools of rhetoric will savour all the sweeter to me.

I think that with that maul of yours you will be able to strike something out of those rocks that you have not got by your own wits from the book shelves of the schoolmen, and that you will have experienced sometimes under the shade of a tree during the heats of midday what you would never have learned in the schools.

I therefore order you to write down those thoughts that have occurred to you, concerning charity, its fruit, and its proper order, so that we may see as if in a mirror what charity is.

To Abbot Rainald

I warned you of the very ills which you declare have befallen you, and you should have been forearmed against what was foreknown so as to have endured them with a lighter heart . . .

This is the burden of souls that are sick, for those that are well do not need to be carried and so are no burden. You must understand that you are especially Abbot of the sad, fainthearted and discontented among your flock. It is by consoling, encouraging and admonishing them that you do your duty and carry your burden and, by carrying your burden, heal those you carry.

If there is anyone so spiritually healthy that he rather helps than is helped by you, you are not so much his Father as his equal, not so much his Abbot as his fellow. Why then do you complain that you find the company of some of those who are with you more of a burden than a comfort?

You were given them as Abbot not to be comforted but to comfort, because you were the strongest of them all, and by God's grace, able to comfort them all without needing to be comforted by any. The greater your burden, the greater will be your gain; the easier your lot, the less your reward.

Giving Thanks for God's Help

In the daily trials and combats arising from the flesh the world and the devil, that are never wanting to those who live devout lives in Christ, you learn by what you experience that man's life on earth is a ceaseless warfare. As often as temptation is overcome, an immoral habit brought under control, an impending danger shunned, the trap of the seducer detected, or when a passion long indulged is finally and perfectly allayed, or a virtue desired and repeatedly sought is ultimately obtained by God's gift, then, in the words of the prophet, 'let thanksgiving and joy resound.'

For every benefit conferred, God is to be praised in his gifts. Otherwise when the time of judgement comes that person will be punished as someone ungrateful who cannot say to God: 'Your statutes were my song in the land of exile.'

Dedication of a Monastic Church

My Brethren, we ought to observe today's festivity all the more devoutly for the reason that it is so specially our own. All the other sacred solemnities which we keep are common to us and the faithful in general. But this is so special to ourselves that if we do not keep it, it will not be kept at all. It is our own feast, because it is the feast of the dedication of our own church.

It is still more our own because it is the feast of our own selves. For what holiness can belong to these dead walls on account of which they should be honoured with a religious solemnity? They are undoubtedly holy, but it is because of your bodies, since they are 'the temples of the Holy Spirit'. Consequently, your souls are sanctified because of the Spirit of God who is in you, your bodies are sanctified because of your souls, and this house is sanctified also because of your bodies.

Many among you have manfully forsaken their vices and sins, and now they offer a stout resistance to the enemy's daily onslaughts; these activities of the spiritual life manifest the indwelling of the Spirit, which is revealed in the practice of charity and the other virtues.

Against Detractors

It has come to my notice that there are some members of our Order who are speaking unfavourably of other Orders, contrary to what the Apostle said, 'Do not pass judgement, before the coming of the Lord'. Who are you to pass judgement on another's servant? Who made you their judges? You glory in the Rule, yet you yourselves do not keep it. The Rule itself has to accord with both Gospel and Apostle, otherwise it would be no Rule at all, since it would be itself untrue. You hypocrite! First remove the log from your own eye. Do you wish to know to which log I am referring? It is the long, large log of pride, which makes you think you are something when in fact you are nothing. You foolishly rejoice in your own soundness, and notwithstanding the log, you scoff at others because of their splinters. The man who shifts his gaze from himself, and is more interested in others' faults than in his own, will be wrenched back and made to take stock of himself; and it will serve him right.

The Kingdom of God is Within You

You retort, 'How can these monks be said to keep the Rule? They wear furs, and they eat meat and fat. Every day they have three or four different dishes, which the Rule forbids, and they leave out the manual work it enjoins. Many points of their Rule they modify or extend or leave out as they like. This is so; no-one could deny it. But look at God's Rule with which St Benedict's regulations agree. It says: 'The Kingdom of God is within you'. The Apostle says: 'It is not food and drink, but righteousness and peace and joy in the Holy Spirit.' And also, 'The kingdom of God consists in power, not in word.' There are people who go clad in tunics and who have nothing to do with furs who, nevertheless, are lacking in humility. Surely humility in furs is better than pride in tunics.

We fill our stomachs with beans and our minds with pride. We condemn rich food as though it were not better to take delicate fare in moderation than to bloat ourselves to belching point with vegetables. Remember that Esau was censured because of lentils, not meat, Adam was condemned for eating fruit not meat.

The Self-opinionated Monk

And what greater pride is there than that one man should try to impose his opinion upon the whole community, as if he alone had the spirit of God? Indeed I am amazed at the impudence of some monks among us, who after they have upset the entire community with their own will, and have irritated us with their impatience, condemned us with their rebelliousness and their bad tempers, desire to aspire, with most fervent prayers, to mystical union with the Lord of all purity.

The centurion begged the Lord not to enter under his roof because of his own unworthiness: and these men would compel the Lord to enter in to their dwelling though it is vile with the filth of such great vices?

'What would you have me do,' such a one will ask. I would first of all have you cleanse your conscience of every stain of anger and quarrelsomeness, of murmuring and bad temper. Then hasten to drive out of your heart whatever goes against peace with your brethren of obedience to your superiors. Then go and prepare yourself with good works, with praise-worthy thoughts, and the sweet-odour of virtues.

The Boaster

His hunger and thirst are for listeners, someone to listen to his boasting, on whom he can pour out all his thoughts, someone he can show what a big man he is. At last the chance to speak comes. He brings forth from his treasury old things and new. He is not shy about producing his opinions; words are bubbling over. He does not wait to be asked. His information comes before any question. He asks the questions; gives the answers; cuts off anyone who tries to speak.

He may have the capacity to help others but that is the least of his concerns. His aim is not to teach you nor to be taught by you, but to show how much he knows. He warmly recommends fasting, urges watching and exalts prayer above all. He will give a long discourse on patience and humility and each of the other virtues – all words, all bragging. He trusts you will draw the conclusion: 'out of the abundance of the heart the mouth speaks'.

The talk takes a lighter turn. He is more in his element here and becomes really eloquent. If you hear him, you will say his mouth has become a fountain of wit, a river of smart talk. He can set the most grave and serious laughing heartily. To say it briefly, when words are many, boasting is not lacking.

Making Excuses

There are many ways of excusing sins. One will say: 'I didn't do it.' Another: 'I did it, but I was perfectly right in doing it.' If it was wrong he may say: 'It isn't all that bad.' If it was decidedly harmful, he can fall back on: 'I meant well.' If the bad intention is too evident he will take refuge in the excuses of Adam and Eve and say someone else led him into it. If a man defends his obvious sins like that, he is hardly likely to fulfil the fifth degree of humility in St Benedict's Rule and 'make known to his Abbot by humble confession the evil thoughts of his heart and the sins he has committed in secret'.

On the Death of Archbishop Malachy at Clairvaux

Dear sons, I feel the deepest compassion for the Irish Church in her great bereavement, and my sympathy for you is all the greater for my realisation of the debt I owe you. The Lord has highly honoured our place with the blessed death of Malachy and enriching it with the treasure of his body. Do not take it ill that he should have his tomb with us, since God out of his abundant mercy has so ordained it that you should have him while he lived and we when he was dead. For both you and us he was a common father, and still is, for this was the wish he expressed to us on his deathbed. Wherefore we embrace you all with deep affection as our true brothers for the sake of this great father of ours. . . .

I exhort you, my brethren, to follow carefully in the footsteps of our father, knowing from daily experience his holy way of life. You will prove yourselves his true sons by manfully keeping his teaching. And as you saw in him a pattern of how you ought to live, live by that pattern, and make more of it than ever.

Even I have been stirred from my sloth and imbued with reverence by the pattern of perfection he set before me. May he so draw me after him that I may run eagerly in the fragrance of his virtues.

On the Death of his Brother Gerard

O, Gerard, what a harvest of joys, what a profusion of blessings is yours. In place of my insignificant person you have the abiding presence of Christ. You have no cause to complain that we have been cut off from you, favoured as you are by the constant presence of the Lord of Majesty and of his heavenly friends. But what do I have in your stead? How I long to know what you think about me, once so uniquely yours, as I sink beneath the weight of cares and afflictions, deprived of the support you lent to my feebleness! Perhaps you still give thought to our needs now that you have plunged into that sea of endless happiness.

But God is love and the deeper one's union with him, the more full one is of love. Your love has not been diminished but only changed; when you were clothed with God you did not divest yourself of concern for us, for God is certainly concerned about us. All that smacks of weakness you have cast away, but not what pertains to love. And since love never comes to an end, you will not forget me for ever.

Living for God Alone

Today, my Brothers, you shall hear something concerning the promise of the Father, the reward of our labour, and the fruit of our captivity. Hard indeed is our captivity, not only that which we endure in common with other men, and which is the general condition of the human race; but also that whereby, in order the more effectually to mortify our wills and to lose our lives in this world, we have bound ourselves by so strict a Rule and such asceticism. Surely a wretched bondage, yet only so if suffered against our will, instead of by free choice.

As it is, however, we have freely offered our liberty to God, and there is no other violence done to our own will than that which comes from the will itself. There must be some cause for this. Indeed there is, my Brothers, and a cause than which none greater can be conceived. I mean the love of God.

All our good works are done not only *for* God, but also *by* God. He is the Author of the good we do, just as he is its Rewarder and its whole Recompense. Is it not by him that we overcome? Yes. For as the sufferings of Christ abound in us, so also *by* Christ does our comfort abound.

Learn to be Merciful

If Christ submitted himself to human misery so that he might not simply know of it, but experience it as well, how much more ought you not to make any change in your condition, but pay attention to what you are, because you are truly full of misery. This is the only way, if you are to become merciful. If you have eyes for the shortcomings of your neighbour and not for your own, no feeling of mercy will arise in you but rather indignation.

You will be more ready to judge than to help, to crush in the spirit of anger than to instruct in the spirit of gentleness. 'You who are spiritual, instruct such a one in the spirit of gentleness,' says the Apostle. His counsel, or rather, his precept, is that you should treat an ailing brother with the same spirit of gentleness with which you would like to be treated yourself in your weakness.

He shows then how to find out the right way to apply this spirit of gentleness: 'Considering yourself lest you also be tempted.'

11

Prayer and Thanksgiving

The following texts fall into three small groups. The first has to do with petition, and is in line with Bernard's emphasis on humility. It means admitting to ourselves and to the God who is our Father that we are not self-sufficient, that we need things we cannot provide for ourselves. We come to him as supplicants, and ultimately it is the Lord himself we are asking for.

The second group is that of thanksgiving, which Bernard always considered important and which he often mentions. We are not to forget even the smallest benefits, he says, for ingratitude is a burning wind which dries up the source of love. Thanksgiving on the other hand moistens the dryness of our hearts and makes them supple. When we find it difficult to pray in times of distractions and aridity, a word of thanksgiving can often bring warmth and life to our coldness.

In the third group he reminds us that God is always with us in times of trouble. Tribulation is the seed of glory, he says, it is a necessary thing. It is the field where the treasure lies hidden.

One wonders if he understands the pain, the anxiety, the heartbreak that can almost tear a person apart? The tension that makes one feel that something is going to snap? It seems that he does, for he quotes: 'The Lord is close to the broken-hearted', 'He is with us even in the valley of the shadow of death'. He is with us every single day until the end of the world. But Bernard does ask if we are with the Lord. Or are we still meditating on our trial?

Ask and You shall Receive

But even you too, if recollected in spirit, if with a mind that is serious and devoid of cares, you enter the house of prayer alone, and standing in the Lord's presence at one of the altars touch the gate of heaven with the hand of holy desire, if in the presence of the choirs of saints where your devotion penetrates – for 'the prayer of the righteous man pierces the heavens' – if you bewail pitiably before them the miseries and misfortunes you endure, and manifest your neediness, and implore their mercy with repeated sighs and groanings too deep for words; if I say you do this, I have confidence in him who said: 'Ask and you shall receive', that if you continue knocking you will not go empty away.

Indeed when you return to us full of grace and love, you will not be able, in the ardour of your spirit, to conceal the gift you have received; you will communicate it without unpopularity, and in the grace that was given to you, you will win the acceptance and even the admiration of everyone.

Seeking the Word in Prayer

Anyone who wishes to pray must choose not only the right place but also the right time. A time of leisure is best and most convenient, the deep silence when others are asleep is particularly suitable, for prayer will then be freer and purer. How secretly prayer goes up in the night, witnessed only by God and the holy Angel who receives it to present it at the heavenly altar. You will not pray aright, if in your prayers you seek anything but the Word, or seek him for anything but the Word; for in him are all things.

In him is the healing for your wounds, help in your need, restoration for your faults, resources for your further growth. In him is all that men should ask or desire, all they need, all that will profit them. There is no need to ask anything else of the Word, for he is all. Even if we seem sometimes to ask for material things, providing that we do so for the sake of the Word, as we should, it is not the things themselves that we are asking for, but him for whose sake we ask them. Those who habitually use all things to find the Word know this.

Thanksgiving

Learn not to be tardy or sluggish in offering thanks, learn to offer thanks for each and every gift. Take careful note, scripture advises, of what is set before you, so that no gift of God, be it great or mediocre or small, will be deprived of due thanksgiving. We are even commended to gather up the fragments, lest they be lost, which means that we are not to forget even the smallest benefits. Is that surely not lost which is given to someone ungrateful? Ingratitude is the soul's enemy, a voiding of merits, dissipation of the virtues, wastage of benefits. Ingratitude is a burning wind that dries up the source of love, the dew of mercy, the streams of grace.

Gladness and Thanksgiving

My advice to you my friends, is to turn aside occasionally from troubled and anxious pondering on the paths you may be treading, and to travel on smoother ways where the gifts of God are quietly savoured. So that the thought of him may give breathing space to you whose consciences are worried. I should like you to experience for yourselves the truth of the words: 'Make the Lord your joy and he will give you what your heart desires'. Sorrow for sin is necessary, but it should not be an endless preoccupation. You must dwell also on the glad remembrance of God's loving kindness, otherwise sadness will harden the heart and lead it more deeply into despair.

You must fix your attention on the ways of God, see how he mitigates the bitterness of the heart that is crushed, how he wins back the timid soul from the abyss of despair, how he consoles the grief-stricken and strengthens the wavering with the sweet caress of his faithful promise.

His loving mercy is greater than all iniquity. 'Think of the Lord with goodness, seek him in simplicity of heart.' You will all the more easily achieve this if you let your minds dwell frequently on the memory of God's bountifulness.

Gratitude for God's Grace

I think it is a good thing to know what I have received from the Lord, so that I may also know what I lack; and I think it my duty to recognise what God has bestowed upon me so that I may know what to pray and sigh for. How can a man return thanks for a gift if he does not know he has received it? Or how can he keep carefully what he has received, if he is not aware of what it is he has received? It is therefore important that we should know how to guard what we have received, and that the grace of God should not be without fruit in our lives.

We should approach by three steps the acquisition of salvation and grace: the steps of humility, faith and fear. It is to the humble man that grace is given, it is with faith that he receives it, and with fear that he guards it. If we would draw the water of wisdom we need the cord which is the Lord's gift; and this is humility on the lips, in the heart, and in our lives. And let our faith be like a water jar, only let it be a big one, so that we may collect much grace with it. Let fear be the cover of the jar, so that the water of wisdom may not be contaminated with vainglory.

God is our Refuge

'You have made the Most High your refuge.' (Psalm 90:2) Brothers, let us fly there frequently: it is a fortified place where no enemy is to be feared. If only we were able to stay there always! But that is not for the present. What is now a refuge will one day be a dwelling place, and an eternal dwelling place. Meanwhile even though we may not stay there, we may however frequently have recourse to it.

In every kind of temptation, in every trial, and in any need of any kind whatever, it is a city of refuge for us, a mother's bosom. The clefts of the rock are ready, the compassionate mercy of our God accessible. If anyone should turn away from this refuge, it will be no wonder if he does not deserve to escape.

There are people who yearn to obtain benefits from the Lord, but perfect love thirsts after the Most High alone, crying out with all the strength of that desire, 'Whom have I in heaven, and what is there upon earth that I desire except you? God is the strength of my heart and my portion for ever. . . . You are good Lord, to those who wait for you, to the soul that seeks you.'[1]

1. From the hymn, *Summa Largitor Praemi*, sung during Lent in Bernard's day.

Tribulation

Let us give thanks to the Father of mercies who is with us in tribulation and consoles us in all our tribulations. A necessary thing, as I have said, is the tribulation which will be changed into glory, as is the sadness which will be turned into joy, a long lasting joy indeed which no-one will take from us, a manifold joy, a full joy. This need is a necessary thing: it produces the crown. Let us not be scornful, Brothers, the seed is tiny, but a great fruit will grow up from it.

The hope of glory lies in tribulation, just as the hope of the fruit lies in the seed. In this way too the Kingdom of God is now within us, a treasure in a clay vessel, in a worthless field. It is there but hidden. Happy is the person who shall find it. The glory is hidden my brothers, concealed from us in tribulation. In this moment eternity lies hidden; in this small thing is hidden a sublime and matchless weight of glory. Let us therefore hasten to buy this field, to buy this treasure lying hidden in the field. Let us count it utter joy when we fall into various tribulations. For Emmanuel, God with us, came down to be near those who are broken-hearted; to be with us in our tribulation.

God is With Us in Trouble

'I am with him in trouble.' When is this if not in the day of our tribulation, the day of our cross. . . . 'The Lord is near to the broken-hearted' and as someone has said: 'Even though I walk through the valley of the shadow of death I will fear no evil, for you are with me'. He is indeed with us every single day until the end of the world. But when shall we be with him?

So now, my sons, let us call out to heaven, and our God will take pity on us. Lift up your heart, lift up your cry, lift up your desires, lift up your way of life, lift up your determination, and let all your expectation come down from above. Cry out to heaven that you may be heard, and your Father who is in heaven will send you help in your distress. He will rescue you from tribulation, he will glorify you in the resurrection.

These are great expectations, but you, great Lord, have promised them. We hope because of your promise, so we dare to say: 'If we cry out with a godly heart then surely you must keep your promise. Amen.'

12

Longing for God

'Seek his face always.' Bernard echoes the Greek Fathers, when he says that even when a soul has found God it will not cease to seek him, because the finding simply increases the desire. Even in heaven there will always be more to discover, 'deeper in and wider out'. So there will be no end to the desire, no end to the search.

It has been said that he belongs to the 'Positive Way', the Cistercian 'Way of Light'. Yet he too, like the brethren he speaks of, experienced God's 'absence', dryness and weariness of soul. In spite of all his monastic observance, he writes, 'My soul is as dry as earth without water'. The desert experience reminds us that union with God is primarily a union of wills. But love too has to do with the will, and the desert is also the meeting place of God and the beloved.

Though it is God who is sought, and not the experience of God, Bernard and his monks long for a personal knowledge of God. Like such spiritual things as loveliness or loneliness, God can only really be known through personal experience. We are not of course speaking of such things as ecstasy, but rather of the knowledge that comes about through love for the Other; a love that is born of commitment made in faith and trust; a trust that is as radical as anything required by John of the Cross.

Seeking God

It is a great good to seek God; in my opinion the soul knows no greater blessing. It is the first of its gifts and the final stage in its progress. This gift is inferior to none and yields place to none. What could be superior to it, when nothing has a higher place? . . . What virtue can be attributed to anyone who does not seek God? What boundary can be set for anyone who does seek him? The psalmist says: 'Seek his face always.' Nor, I think, will a soul cease to seek him even when it has found him.

It is not with steps of the feet that God is sought but with the desire of the heart; and when the soul happily finds him its desire is not quenched but kindled . . . there will be a fulness of joy, but there will be no end to desire, and therefore no end to the search.

Think if you can, of this eagerness to see God as not caused by his absence, for he is always present; and think of the desire for God as without fear of failure, for grace is abundantly present.

Dryness

I am not ashamed to admit that very often I myself, especially in the early days of my conversion, experienced coldness and hardness of heart, while deep in my being I sought for him whom I longed to love. I could not yet love him since I had not yet really found him; at best my love was less than it should have been, and for that very reason I sought to increase it, for I would not have sought him if I did not already love him to some degree. I sought him that in him my numbed and languid spirit might find warmth and repose, for nowhere could I find a friend to help me, whose love would thaw the wintery cold that chilled my inward being, and bring back again the feeling of spring-like bliss and spiritual delight.

But my weariness only increased, my soul melted away for sorrow, even to the verge of despair. All I could do was to repeat softly to myself: 'Who can stand before his cold?' Then at times when I least expected, at the word of a good or holy man, at the memory of a dead or absent friend, he set his wind blowing and the waters flowing. For me there was no anointing, but rather the experience that came through another's mediation.

The Complaint of the Spouse

Let us suppose that those whom I have called the friends of the Bridegroom have come on a visit to greet the Spouse. Finding her discontented they wonder what the cause can be and ask her: 'What has happened? Are you afraid you will be called upon to answer for the sins of your past life which you hoped had been forgiven?' 'No indeed, but I cannot rest until he kisses me with the kiss of his Mouth. I am not ungrateful but – I love.

'For many years for his sake, I have been careful to lead a chaste and sober life; I have applied myself to spiritual reading; I have resisted my unruly passions; I have watched against temptation; and have been constant in prayer. As far as I could I have lived a good community life, and been obedient . . . I have not coveted my neighbour's goods, but rather given him my own and myself with them. In the sweat of my brow have I eaten my bread. Yet in all these exercises I have felt nothing save the monotonous drudgery of routine, unseasoned with sweetness. I am perhaps, in some way faithfully observing the commandments, yet even in that observance, my soul is as dry as earth without water. Let him, I beg, "Kiss me with the kiss of his mouth".'

Longing for the Holy Spirit

Many of you, as I recall, in our private conversations, complain of this languor and dryness of soul, this heaviness and dullness of mind, devoid of the power to penetrate the profound and hidden truths of God, devoid too, entirely or for the most part, of the sweetness of the Spirit. What is that my Brothers, but a longing to be kissed?

Plainly, such persons are sighing and yearning after the Spirit of wisdom and insight. Insight that they may attain to what they long for, wisdom in order to savour what the mind apprehends. With such feelings the prophet prayed when he said, 'My soul will feast most richly, on my lips a song of joy and in my mouth, praise.'

The kiss of the Holy Spirit was surely what he sought for, that kiss at whose touch the lips are so bedewed with the richness of spiritual grace; thus was fulfilled his wish, spoken in another context: 'Let my mouth be filled with your praise, that I may sing of your glory, of your splendour all the day long'. Then no sooner has he tasted than he cries out, 'How great is the abundance of your goodness Lord, reserved for those who revere you.'

The Holy Spirit: the Kiss

'Let him kiss me with the kiss of his mouth.' Do you wish to see the newly-chosen bride receiving this unprecedented kiss, given not by the mouth but by the kiss of the mouth? Then look at Jesus in the presence of his Apostles: 'He breathed on them, and he said, "Receive the Holy Spirit".' That favour given to the newly chosen Church, was indeed a kiss. 'That?' you say. 'That corporal breathing?' O no, but rather the invisible Spirit, who is so bestowed in that breath of the Lord that he is understood to proceed from him equally as from the Father; truly the kiss is common both to the Father who kisses, and to the Son who is kissed.

So the Bride is satisfied to receive the kiss of the Bridegroom, though she be not kissed with his mouth. For her it is no mean thing to be kissed by the kiss, because this is nothing less than the gift of the Holy Spirit. If, the Father is he who kisses, and the Son is he who is kissed, then it cannot be wrong to see in the kiss the Holy Spirit, for he is the imperturbable peace of the Father and the Son, their unshakable bond, their undivided love, their indivisible unity.

Knowing the Trinity

When the Son said: 'No-one knows the Son except the Father, just as no-one knows the Father except the Son,' he added: 'and those to whom the Son chooses to reveal him.' But the Bride has no doubt that if he will reveal himself to anybody, it will be to her. Therefore, she dares to ask for this kiss. She asks for that Spirit in whom both the Father and the Son will reveal themselves to her. For it is not possible that one of these could be known without the other.

When the Bride asks for the kiss therefore, she asks to be filled with the grace of this threefold knowledge. She asks to be filled to the utmost capacity of mortal flesh. But it is the Son whom she approaches, since it is by him it is to be revealed, and to whom he wills. And it is certain that he makes this revelation through the kiss, that is through the Holy Spirit.

It is by giving the Spirit, through whom he reveals, that he shows us himself. . . . Furthermore, this revelation which is made through the Holy Spirit, not only conveys the light of knowledge but also lights the fire of love, as St Paul testifies: 'The love of God has been poured into our hearts by the Holy Spirit which has been given to us.'

The Man of Desires   I

If any of us, like the holy prophet, find that it is good to cling close to God, and – that I may make my meaning clear – if any of us is so filled with desire that he wants to depart and to be with Christ, with a desire that is intense, with a thirst ever burning, with an application that never flags, he will certainly meet the Word in the guise of a Bridegroom on whatever day he comes.

At such an hour he will find himself locked, interiorly, in the arms of wisdom; he will experience how sweet divine love is as it flows into his heart. His heart's desire will be given to him, even while still a pilgrim on earth, though not in its fulness and only for a time, a short time. For when after vigils and a great deal of tears, he who was sought presents himself, suddenly he is gone again, just when we think we hold him fast. But he will present himself anew to the soul that pursues him with tears, he will allow himself to be taken hold of but not detained, for suddenly for a second time he flees from between our hands.

The Man of Desires II

And if the fervent soul persists with prayers and tears, the Bridegroom will return each time and not defraud him of his express desire, but only to disappear soon again and not to return again unless he is sought for with all one's heart. And so, even in this body we can often enjoy the happiness of the Bridegroom's presence, but it is a happiness that is never complete because the joy of his visit is followed by the pain of his departure. The beloved has no choice but to endure this state until the hour when she lays down the body's weary weight, and raised aloft by the wings of desire, freely traverses the meadows of contemplation, and in spirit follows the One she loves without restraint wherever he goes.

Faith and Desire

Because we cannot yet contemplate the reality of God nor fully embrace him by love, he feeds us on that hidden manna of which the Apostle says: 'Your life is hid with Christ in God', allowing us to taste him by faith and seek him by desire. By these two, faith in him and desire for him, we are brought a second time from a state of nothingness to a state of being, and we begin to be once more, after a fashion, creatures of God, to pass at last into the perfect man, 'into the measure of the age of the fulness of Christ'.

And this will come about when faith will be turned into understanding or when the justice that arises from faith is transformed into the judgement that comes from full knowledge, and the desire experienced in exile is changed into fulness of love.

If faith in God and desire for him start the exile off on the way, they culminate in understanding and love when he is there. As faith leads to full knowledge, so desire leads to perfect love. If you do not desire God ardently, you will not love him perfectly. Understanding is therefore the fruit of faith, and perfect love the fruit of desire.

Visits of the Word

I want to tell you of my own experience as I promised. I admit that the Word has also come to me – and has come many times. But although he has come to me, I have never been conscious of the moment of his coming. I perceived his presence, I remembered afterwards that he had been with me; sometimes I had a presentiment that he would come, but I was never conscious of his coming or his going. And where he comes from when he visits my soul, and where he goes, and by what means he enters and goes out, I admit that I do not know even now.

The coming of the Word was not perceptible to my eyes, nor to my ears; his coming was not tasted by the mouth, nor could he be known by the sense of touch. How then did he enter? Perhaps he did not enter because he does not come from outside? Yet he does not come from within me, for he is good, and I know there is no good in me. If I looked outside myself, I saw him stretching away beyond the furthest I could see; and if I looked within, he was yet further within. Then I knew the truth of what I had read, 'In him we live and move and have our being'. And blessed is the man in whom he has his being, who lives for the Word and is moved by him.

The Presence of the Word

You ask then how I knew he was present when his ways can in no way be traced? He is life and power, and as soon as he enters in, he awakens my slumbering soul. He stirs and soothes and pierces my heart, for before it was hard as stone, and diseased. So he has begun to pluck out and destroy, to build up and to plant, to water dry places and illumine dark ones; to open what was closed and to warm what was cold, so that my soul may bless the Lord, and all that is within me may praise his holy name.

So when the Word came to me, he never made known his coming by any signs, not by sight, not by sound, not by touch. It was not by any movement of his that I perceived his coming; only by the movement of my heart did I perceive his presence. I knew the power of his might because my faults were put to flight and my human yearnings brought into subjection. But when he has left me, all these spiritual powers become weak and faint and begin to grow cold. As often as he slips away from me, so often shall I call him back. As long as I live the word 'return', for the recall of the Word, will be on my lips.

Enjoying the Word

There may be someone who will ask me, 'What does it mean to enjoy the Word?' I would answer that he must find someone who has experience of it and ask him. Do you suppose that if I had had that experience I could describe it to you?

I may have been granted this experience but I do not speak of it. I have made allowance in what I have said, so that you could understand me. Oh, whoever is curious to know what it means to enjoy the Word, make ready your heart, not your ear! The tongue does not teach this, grace does. It is hidden from the wise and prudent, and revealed to children.

Humility, my brothers, is a great virtue, great and sublime. It can attain to what it cannot learn; it is counted worthy to possess what it has not the power to possess; it is worthy to conceive by the Word and from the Word, what it cannot explain in words.

Why is this? Not because it deserves to do so, but because it pleases the Father of the Word, the Bridegroom of the soul, Jesus Christ our Lord who is God above all, blessed for ever. Amen.

To Love with the Whole Heart

The stream of love does not flow equally from her who loves and from him who is love, the soul and the Word, the Bride and the Bridegroom, the Creator and the creature – any more than a thirsty man can be compared to a fountain. Will the Bride's vow then perish because she cannot equal the brightness of the sun, and the charity of him who is Charity itself? No. Although the creature loves less, being a lesser being, yet if it loves with its whole heart nothing is lacking, for it has given all.

Such love, as I have said is marriage, for a soul cannot love like this and not be beloved; complete and perfect marriage consists in the exchange of love. No-one can doubt that the soul is first loved, and loved more intensely by the Word; for it is anticipated and surpassed in its love. Happy the soul who is permitted to be anticipated in blessedness so sweet.

For it is nothing other than love, holy and chaste, full of sweetness and delight, love utterly serene and true, mutual and deep, which joins two beings, not in one flesh, but in one spirit, making them no longer two but one.

13

The Day

So often our thoughts stop short of the object of all our striving – heaven, and all it implies: the close presence and sight of God, the companionship of those who have gone on before. Bernard, commenting on the 'Canticle', writes magnificently of that Day on which the sun never sets on a land that is richer and more fertile than any we have ever known. A place where there is no fear, no more violence or squalor or want, no more oppression or misery.

It will be a day without evening, but which had its dawn when the Virgin conceived God in her womb by the power of the Holy Spirit. It had its sunrise early on that morning when night was swallowed up in the victory of the Resurrection. Bernard writes of its noontime: 'Lord, tell me where you pasture your flock at noontide, show me this place that I too may gaze upon you in your light and your beauty, . . . Lord, I do seek your face, your face which is the noontide.'

It is a day, the Day which unites heaven and earth.

Heaven

The sun, however, even though it increases in warmth and strength, though it extends its rays over the whole course of our mortal loves – for it will be with us even to the end of the world – it will not attain to its noontide splendour, nor be seen here below in that fulness which it will show hereafter. O true noontide, fulness of warmth and light, trysting place of the sun; noontide that blots out the shadows, that dries up the marshes, that banishes evil odours! O perpetual solstice, day that will never decline to evening! O noontide light, with your springtime freshness, your summer-like gracefulness, your autumnal fruitfulness and your winter of quiescence and leisure.

All things here below fall short of perfection, many are beyond the reach of my desires, and nothing is safe. When will you fill me with the joy of your presence? Lord, I do seek your face. Your face is the noontide. Tell me where you pasture your flock, where you make it lie down at noon. Show me this place, where there is so much brightness and peace and fulness, so that just as Jacob while still in this life saw the Lord face to face, I too may merit the grace of contemplating you in your light and beauty.

The Mystical Noontide

Let us make haste, my Sons, let us make haste to a place that is safer, to a pasture that is sweeter, to a land that is richer and more fertile. To a place where we may dwell without fear, where we may abound and never want, where we may feast and never weary. O Lord of Hosts, you feed in security and with fairness all who dwell in that place, you who are at the same time the Lord of armies and shepherd of sheep. You feed your flock therefore and at the same time make them rest, but not here below.

'Show me where you pasture your flock, where you make it lie down at noon', that is the whole day long: for that noon is a day that knows no evening. So a day in your courts is better than a thousand elsewhere, because its sun never sets. But perhaps it had a sunrise when that holy day first dawned upon us through the tender mercy of our God, in which the Rising Sun visited us from heaven. Truly then we received your mercy, O God, when as you rose out of the shadow of death, the morning light shone over us, and in the dawn we saw the glory of God.

The Day

The dawning of this day began when the Sun of righteousness was announced to the earth by the Archangel Gabriel; when the Virgin conceived God in her womb by the power of the Holy Spirit, and still remaining a virgin gave birth to him; and it continued as long as he was seen on earth and lived among men. For during all that time only a feeble light, just like the dusk of dawn, was visible, so that almost the whole world failed to realise that daytime for mankind had come.

The dawn then, was the whole life of Christ upon earth, until he died and rose again to put the dawn to flight by the clearer light of his glorious presence. With the coming of sunrise, night was swallowed up in victory. And so we are told that very early on the Sunday morning, just after sunrise, they came to the tomb. Surely it was morning when the Sun had risen? But the resurrection endowed it with a new beauty, with a more serene light than usual, because though we once knew him according to the flesh, we know him thus no longer. He shook off the frailties of the flesh like cloudlets and put on the robe of glory. Since then the Sun is risen indeed and has gradually poured down its rays over the earth.

Epilogue

Bernard's great contribution was to remind people that God not only came into this world at the incarnation and will come again at the end of time, but that he also comes daily, by grace, into the hearts of all those who will welcome him. His work of salvation has never halted and it will continue as long as there are men and women to work out their salvation. This work still goes on in our world, the modern world we know, which is sinful, greedy, and often too proud to be honest with itself. But it is a world where there are many who are hurt, lost, seeking, longing for they know not what. (That 'I don't know what' for which John of the Cross was prepared to gamble his all.)

It is this world which Bernard also knew and wrote about, for like Jesus he was concerned with human nature, which does not change very much. But he had grasped the fact that wherever there is a spark of free-will, wherever there is an atom of love, there also is the capacity, the potential for union with the God for whom we were made and without whom no individual will be complete. Bernard reminds us that we are not on our own; it is in this world of luxury and squalor, of violence and great beauty, of suffering and indescribable love, that Christ seeks the sinners he came to save, that he knocks on the hearts of ordinary people. If they will open to him, then together he and they may make the living of the ups and downs of human life the vehicle of salvation, and life as a fully human being and as a follower of Christ may become one and the same. It is a life's work but it results in human completeness and a share in the glorious life and love of the Blessed Trinity.

God's glory is in living men and women and full life for

them is in the vision of God. It is this kind of life and union with God – being fully human and being fully Christian – that was preached and practised by St Bernard of Clairvaux.

Sources

Source references are abbreviated as follows:

CF1   *The Works of Bernard of Clairvaux: Treatises I*, Cistercian Fathers Series no 1. (Cistercian Publications, Massachusetts, 1970)

CF4   *The Works of Bernard of Clairvaux: On the Song of Sons I*, Cistercian Fathers Series no 4, trans. Kilian Walsh OCSO. (Cistercian Publications, Massachusetts, 1971)

CF7   *The Works of Bernard of Clairvaux: On the Song of Songs II*, Cistercian Fathers Series no 7, trans. Kilian Walsh OCSO (Cistercian Publications, Michigan, 1983)

CF31 *The Works of Bernard of Clairvaux: On the Song of Songs III*, Cistercian Fathers Series no 31, trans, Kilian Walsh OCSO & Irene Edmonds. (Cistercian Publications, Michigan, 1974)

CF40 *The Works of Bernard of Clairvaux: On the Song of Songs IV*, Cistercian Fathers Series no 40, trans. Irene Edmonds. (Cistercian Publications, Michigan, 1980)

CF13 *The Works of Bernard of Clairvaux: Treatise II*, Cistercian Fathers Series no 13. (Cistercian Publications Consortium Press, Washington DC, 1974)

CF19 *The Works of Bernard of Clairvaux: Treatises III*, Cistercian Fathers Series no 19. trans. D. O'Donovan OCSO. (Cistercian Publications, Michigan, 1977)

CF25 *The Works of Bernard of Clairvaux: Sermons on Conversion*, Cistercian Fathers Series no 25, trans. Marie-Bernard Said OSB. (Cistercian Publications, Michigan, 1981)

CS9   *Thomas Merton on St Bernard*, Cistercian Studies Series no 9. (Mowbray, London, 1980)

LG   *On Loving God by Bernard of Clairvaux*, Hugh Martin (ed). (SCM Press, London, 1959)

BCY   *St Bernard on the Christian Year*. (Mowbray, London, 1954)

LI   *St Bernard's Sermons for the Seasons and Principal Festivals of the Year*, Vol I. (Browne & Nolan, Dublin, 1921)

LII	*ibid*, Vol II. (Browne & Nolan. Dublin, 1923)
LIII	*ibid*, Vol III. (Browne & Nolan. Dublin, 1925)
CII	*St Bernard's Sermons on the Canticle of Canticles*. Vol II. (Browne & Nolan, Dublin 1920).
LB	*The Letters of St Bernard of Clairvaux*, trans. Bruno Scott James. (Burns & Oates, London, 1953)
AT	Author's translation

Works of St Bernard are abbreviated as follows:

SoS	On Song of Songs
Lov God	On Loving God
Conv	On Conversion
Pre	On Precept and Dispensation
GVM	On Glories of the Virgin Mother
Ps 90	On Psalm 90
Ad	Sermons for Advent
Nat	Sermons for Christmas
Pent	Sermon for Pentecost
Nat BVM	For Birthday of the Blessed Virgin
Hum	Steps of Humility and Pride
Gra	Grace and Free-choice
Apol	Apologia
Lett	Letters

1 The Mystery of Christ

What the Blessed Trinity has Done for Us   Pent II, 2; LII 297
Charity is the Law of God   Lett 12, 4; LB 44
The Law of the Slave   Lett, 12, 5; LB 44
Christ our Saviour   Ad VII; LI 51 ff
Our Need of Christ   Ad VII; LI 51 ff.
The Time of our Saviour's Coming   Ad I; AT
The Road by which the Saviour Comes   Ad I; AT
The Kindness of God   Ad I; LI 10
Why the Son of God Came to Us   Ad I; LI 10 & 17.

2 Love

Love   SoS 83.4; CF40 184
How God Should be Loved   Lov God VI 16; CF13 109
Why We Should Love God   Lov God I; LG 16
Christ First Loved Us   SoS 20.2; CF4 148
How We Ought to Love Christ   SoS 20.4; CF4 149
Degrees of Love   SoS 83 5; CF40 184 ff.

True Love   Lov God VII 17; CF13 110
Steps in our Love for God   Lett 12 8; LB 46

3   Our Lady

Mary our Advocate   Ad II; LI 20 ff
The Annunciation   GVM IV 8; LI 124
Mary's Consent   GVM IV 8; LI 126
Star of the Sea   GVM II; AT
The Second Eve   Nat BVM 6; LIII 286
For Our Lady's Birthday   Nat BVM 6; LIII 284
Mary gives us Jesus our Brother   Nat BVM 7; LIII 288
Mary, the Garden   Nat BVM 6, 7; LIII 287 ff

4   Made in God's Image and Likeness

The Image and Likeness   SoS 80 2; CF40 146
The Capacity for God   SoS 80 3, 4; CF40 146 ff
Lord, Who is Like You?   SoS 82 7; CF40 178
The Likeness and the Vision   SoS 82 8; CF40 179
Made in God's Image and Likeness   Gra IX; CF19 84
Free Choice   SoS 81 6; CF40 162
Simplicity   SoS 81 2; CS9 111 ff
Our Unlikeness to God   SoS 82 2; CS9 112 ff

5   Conversion

Come Home Without Fear   SoS 83, 1; CF40 180–1
Conversion I   Conv 1, 24; CF25 31, 35
Conversion II   Conv 5, 7, 8, 10; CF25 37, 44
Conversion III   Conv 11, 12; CF25 45–6
The Desire for Contemplation   Conv 23, 24, 25; CF25 58, 61
The Soul Wedded to the Word   SoS 83, 23; CF40 182

6   Humility

A Deep Heart   Hum 15, 16, 17; CF13, 43, 45
Self-Knowledge   SoS 37.1; CS9 123 – 4
Humility of Heart   Ad IV; LI 35
Humiliations   Lett, 90, 11; LB 134
Three Degrees of Truth   Hum 6, 9; CF13, 34, 37
Blessed are the Merciful   Conv 29; CF25 65
The Taste of Wisdom   SoS 85 7, 8; CF40 202, 204

7 · Our Need for God's Help

Renewal   SoS 21 6; CF7 8
God Gives Us the Power   SoS 84 3; CF40 190
The Search for God   SoS 84 5; CF40 191–2
Returning to God   SoS 84 6; CF40 192–3
The Goodness of God   Lett 90 6; LB 132
To be Re-formed by the Word   SoS 83 2; CF40 181–2
The Help of the Word   SoS 85 5; CF40 200–1
The Bride of the Word   SoS 85 12; CF40 208–9

8 Finding God in the Church

The Church   SoS 12, 11; CF4 86
The Robe of Christ   Apol. III, 6; CF1 40–1
The Robe of Unity   Apol. IV, 7–9; CF1 41, 44
The Lord Jesus   SoS 20. 1; CF4 147, 149
Human Affection for Christ   SoS 20. 6; CF4 152
God's Self-emptying   SoS 11, 7; CF4 74, 75
The Three Unions   Nat III, 7, 9, 10; LI 337, 340
Reconciliation   Epiph. I. 1–4; BCY 38–9

9 The Lord Jesus

The Name of Jesus   SoS 15. 6; CF4 110
The Healing Power of the Name of Jesus   SoS 15. 8; CF4 111
I Am the Way   Hum I. 1; CF13 29
Christ Feeds Us and is Fed by Us   SoS 71. 4, 5; CF40 51–2
Lent with the Church   Lent I, 1, 2; BCY 64–5
The Palm Sunday Procession   Pa I 2; LII 113, 114
The Sufferings of Christ   SoS 43.3; CF7 221–2
The Wounds of Christ   SoS 61. 3. 4; CII 196
Resurrection   Res I; BCY 92–3
Passing Beyond   SoS 79.3; CF40 139
Christ our Companion   SoS 32.4; CF7 136–7
The Gift of the Spirit   Lett 109; AT
Faith   Res. II; AT
St Peter and St Paul   Sts P & P I; LIII 194, 196
The Pharisee and the Publican   Annum III 10; LIII 171–2
The Holy Angels   St. Michael. I. 6; LIII 320
Guardian Angels   Ps 90. 12, 6; CF25 217
The Cross   St. And. I; BCY 112

10 *The Cistercian Way of Life*

The Cistercian Way Lett 151.2; LB 220
Monastic Life: a Second Baptism Pre XVII, 54; CF I 144
To the Parents of a Novice Lett 112; LB 169
Christ's Yoke is Easy Lett 75.2; LB 104
To Henry Murdac Lett. 107; LB 155
Clairvaux Lett 67; LB 91
To Aelred of Rievaulx Lett 177; LB 246
To Abbot Rainald Lett 76. 1; LB 106
Giving Thanks for God's Help SoS 1.9; CF4 5–6
Dedication of a Monastic Church Ded. I; LII 385
Against Detractors Apol V 10, 11; CFI 45–6
The Kingdom of God is Within You Apol VI 12; CFI 46, 48
The Self-opinionated Monk SoS 46.6; AT
The Boaster Hum XIII 41; CFB 69
Making Excuses Hum XVII 45; CF13 73
On the Death of Archbishop Malachy at Clairvaux
  Lett 386. 3; LB 456
On the Death of his Brother Gerard SoS 26.5; CF7 63
Living for God Alone Ps 90. 9; LI 210
Learn to be Merciful Hum IV 13; CF13 41

11 *Prayer and Thanksgiving*

Ask and You shall Receive SoS 49. 3; CF31 23
Seeking the Word in Prayer SoS 86. 3; CF40 213–14
Thanksgiving SoS 51. 6; CF31 44–5
Gladness and Thanksgiving SoS 11, 2; CF4 70
Gratitude for God's Grace Lett 417; LB 485
God is our Refuge Ps 90. 9. 7; CF25 189–90
Tribulation Ps 90 17. 3; CF25 255–6
God is With Us in Trouble Ps 90. 16: 2, 4; CF25 248–9

12 *Longing for God*

Seeking God SoS 84. 1; CF40 188
Dryness SoS 14. 6; CF4 102
The Complaint of the Spouse SoS 9. 1, 2; CF4 53–4
Longing for the Holy Spirit SoS 9. 3; CF4 55
The Holy Spirit: the Kiss SoS 8, 2; CF4 46
Knowing the Trinity SoS 8. 3, 5; CF4 46–7
The Man of Desires I SoS 32, 2; CF7 135
The Man of Desires II SoS 32. 2; CF7 135
Faith and Desire Lett 19. 2; LB 53

Visits of the Word   SoS 74. 5; CF40 89–90
The Presence of the Word   SoS 74. 6, 7; CF40 91
Enjoying the Word   SoS 85. 14; CF40 210
To Love with the Whole Heart   SoS 83. 6; CF40 186

13   The Day

Heaven   SoS 33, 6, 7; CF7 149–50
The Mystical Noontide   SoS 33. 4; CF7 147
The Day   SoS 32, 5, 6; CF7 148–9